These Hills, My Home

A Buffalo River Story

Billie Touchstone Hardaway

For you shall go out in joy,
and be led forth in peace;
the mountains and the hills before you
shall break forth into singing,
and all the trees of the field
shall clap their hands.
—Isaiah 55:12

Dedicated in loving memory to my late husband and father of my children, Hal Theo Hardaway. He spent many lonely days and nights, with only the old tom cat for company, while I searched the hills for a story.

Billie Touchstone Hardaway -- 1980

CONTENTS

These Hills, My Home

I

Introduction

The Ozarks of Northwest Arkansas represent the very best in panoramic scenery and warmhearted folks who just can't be anything but outstanding, living in such a place. The high bluffs, fertile valleys, rushing creeks and the famous Buffalo National River made the area truly a Mecca of the Seventies and certainly the Eighties as well.

I have been a part of These Hills since 1969 and my life has taken on an unexplained richness and quality since then. Perhaps it is partly because of a very warm friend by the name of Frank Villines.

I met Frank in the fall of 1970, his 86th year, when the timber wore its loveliest colors. His sparkling blue eyes and witty expressions captured my interest to learn more about this unusual man, who had lived most of those years on "Ole Buffalo." I knew he could tell me much about this rough and beautiful part of the Ozarks and I vowed to write a book about him and his hills of Newton County.

The first edition of that book was published in 1972, a "hurry up" affair as so many of the wonderful people in the book were quite old and I feared they might go on "beyond the river" before I could finish it. Now, eight years later, so much more needs to be added to the "little book". I have met hundreds of people who have helped me to know these hills more intimately. Then, too, I know that River which is so captivating to Frank Villines and myself, a little better. She holds one to her bosom as a mother holds a child and is capable of comforting the most confused, heartsick soul.

There is a magic in that "creek", as it is locally called, and that magic becomes a part of all who visit her and dream on her pebbly banks.

After a sellout of three printings of that first edition, I realize that many must love These Hills and Ole Buffalo as much as I since people from nearly every state have bought the little book, whose cover depicts a man carrying a wildcat on his back.

Frank and I have ridden thousands of miles yelling to each other above the roar of an old truck while bouncing over rubboard roads. Often, our travels were in the rain and over ice and snow covered roads and fog hugged the mountains so fiercely that it choked out the sunlight. But in spite of it all, we were able to see places and talk with people, all of which brought about the conclusion of "the book."

We have stood in the frosty October morning and watched Ross Villines, Frank's cousin, make "lasses" at Ponca and walked the narrow goat trail of Center Point Bluff (popularly known as Big Bluff) to its very end. We ate gritted bread and fried meat on the banks of Ole Buffalo and searched out a wild onion the size of a banty egg to complete the delicious meal, prepared by Frank. **We** drank steaming cups of coffee from a thermos while Frank told me so much and I wrote it in my mind, on my pad and in my heart.

Really, the book is Frank's, for without his uncanny memory, his sense of humor, his physical stamina and determination to finish something started, I could not have written it. The book has been his most constant companion and he has sold thousands from his hip pocket and through the mail.

Also, to Tommy House, goes my heartfelt appreciation for the many areas of research he provided. Tommy is a Villines descendant born and reared in Newton County.

Frank tells an exquisite yarn about the fellow who had lived in the Ozarks all his life. He died and went to Heaven where he saw streets of gold. However, when springtime in the Ozarks came, they had to chain this gentlemen to keep him from returning. Every spring, this had to be done. Since living in the Ozarks of northwest Arkansas for the past ten years, I can understand how he must have felt.

This revised and expanded edition of my "love story" about Frank Villines, his hills, his river and his people, is presented straight from my heart, as was the first edition.

Springtime in the Ozarks — 1980 Billie Touchstone Hardaway

Sarah Thomas & Frank Villines 1902

Addie Raney, Frank Villines, Leness House and Minnie Strickland —1914

II

IN THE BEGINNING...

So and no otherwise — so and no otherwise — Hillmen desire their hills!
— Rudyard Kipling

Abraham Villines, the illustrious progenitor of all the Newton County Villines, was born about 1772. He, like his biblical namesake, was the patriarch of his clan.

The surname "Villines" (also spelled Verline, Verlain, Velines, Veline, and Vallian) is very likely French Hugenot (French protestants of the 16th and 17th century) origin. They immigrated to America about 1700, settling first in Virginia and then going on to North Carolina.

The Villines in North Carolina were wealthy tobacco farmers. However, an economic depression struck the area, due either to a drought or a tax burden — the record does not say, except that their lands were placed in receivership.

Abraham knew they could not bear up under the adversity of their lands being confiscated, and so he and his family settled up the estate in North Carolina and moved to Tennessee.

He began to hear romantic rumors from some of his adventurous Tennessee kinspeople who had gone to northwest Arkansas on a two year expedition. The hunters eventually camped on a big flat rock which covered several hundred feet near the Buffalo River. Such a rock exists on Sneed Creek in Newton County (called "Rocky Bottom") where some of the Villines later settled. The hunters' story is that they stayed a week on the rock, survived an attack by a panther, hunted to their hearts content and hurried back to Tennessee to bring their families to this unspoiled paradise. Abraham gave serious thought to the stories brought back by his Tennessee relatives before making the decision to come to Arkansas. Then, in about the year 1837, he led his people to Arkansas. It has been told time and again that the Villines caravan was the richest ever to come to Arkansas. One

5

cannot say this positively, since they had experienced devastation of their property rights. But it can be said with certainty that the caravan must have been very rich indeed in feverish anticipation, hopes and desires for a better way of life. And then, perhaps they were able to retain many of their material possessions.

The caravan included many ox drawn wagons, heavily laden with household furnishings and supplies to see them through their first winter, beef cattle, milk cows and poultry in hand made crates. Geese were tolled with com from the aprons of young girls.

It is believed that families other than Villines were in that same caravan since the Census Records reveal their presence in Carroll County (later Newton County) in 1840 and that they had come from North Carolina and Tennessee.

The slaves had been sold; that is, all except one. Piety (called Pied by some) remained with the Villines until her death. She had been a wedding gift to Hezekiah and Elizabeth Penn Villines from Abraham when she was only ten years old. Before the end of her life, she contributed much to that family above and beyond the call of duty of a freed slave.

Elizabeth offered Piety her freedom before the trip south but Piety, then about twenty years of age, cried and begged to stay with them. It has been related many times how she was never considered a slave, but rather a companion to Elizabeth who helped with the children's care and the housework. As the story goes, Elizabeth and Piety had an agreement as they grew older; that if one or the other were unable to care for herself, they would care for each other. And apparently, they did this. It was Elizabeth who finally became feeble and senile and Aunt Piety, out of love and the promise, who took care of her until her death.

The family built a small house for Aunt Piety near the road so she could pass her last days sitting on the porch watching the goings and comings of those she had loved and for whom she had cared for more than fifty years.

Abraham knew he would not need slaves in the new and mountainous country and legend has it that he had never been comfortable owning human chattels anyway. He and his large family could work the patches and small cleared fields without the help of slaves.

With Abraham was his bride of a few years, Martha. His first wife and mother of his children, Nancy McKissack Villines, had died and her estate settled years before. Martha might have been Nancy's sister. Abraham and Martha, both in their later years, did not have children.

There is controversy as to the route they took. Some think they came through Alabama, crossing the great river with much effort and loss of some of their possessions; others say they travelled through Tennessee, down through Missouri and then through Old Carrollton and over the mountains to the Buffalo River area. The latter seems more likely since it is believed that Hezekiah and his family joined the Villines caravan as it came through Missouri.

Abraham's children, though grown and some married with families, came with their father to this "new land." They were: Hezekiah (married to Elizabeth Penn), Hosea, age 16, Nathanial, age 20, Virginia, age 21 and Copeland, age 13. Another son, William, remained in North Carolina, where he was a slave dealer, and during the Civil War, a Confederate Officer.

Abraham and his unmarried children and Martha settled on Buffalo under "Big Bluff." Across the river was a good spring of water gushing from beneath giant beechnut trees which grew abundantly along the river. Above the spring was a grassy knoll which provided an excellent site for a house, where it would be safe from the unpredictable river in flood stage. Hezekiah and the others moved on up the river near the mouth of Running Creek, settling in choice locations.

A young man by the name of John Penn was also in the caravan. It is believed this was Elizabeth's brother.

It has been related that the first winter was spent in a tent with an open end for a fireplace. A "tent" was then built of slabs or boards set on end, fastened at the top with wooden pins against poles or logs resting on four forks or posts sunk into the ground.

The nearest grist mill was near Rogers, Arkansas and when Hezekiah went to the mill, the trip took several days. Elizabeth would sit up all night to keep the wild animals from entering the tent.

The old home place where Abraham and his family first settled fell to the youngest son, Copeland, who lived there and raised twelve children. He was the grandfather of Frank Villnes of this book. Copeland married Jincy Reeves.

The scenery which greeted the weary, anxious travelers must indeed have been a sight to behold, so beautiful and untouched were the canyons, caves and coves, the rugged, steep hills reaching skyward from the Buffalo River which was to be the very lifeline of the little caravan and their many descendants to come after them.

The Buffalo carved through the mountains over eons of time and produced rich, fertile valleys. Cedar trees, big around as three men, rose majestically from the river's banks and cane brakes. Game of every kind abounded and Abraham knew he had made a wise decision. And like the Abraham before him, he thanked his Maker for the paradise which greeted them and for the safe journey.

Hezekiah, for some time had suffered from a cough which made him ill and very weak. But he felt that with the arrival to their new home he would be better. Then, too, he remembered that "Hezekiah" was a Hebrew name meaning "God Strengthens." But, for his own reasons, God did not strengthen Hezekiah and, though in his forties, he was laid to rest. There was grieving but life went on. The Villines clan settled in, constructing sturdy log cabins and clearing plots for farming. And they multiplied!

The year 1860 was a good one for the county and following is an agricultural report showing the productivity. There were now five hundred fifty-nine households in Newton County, and a goodly percentage of them had the name Villines.

Children born to Hezekiah and Elizabeth Penn Villines:

Artist's conception of Jefferson Villines, son of Hezekiah and Elizabeth Penn
Villines, taken from an old tin type photograph (before Civil War)

NAME	BORN	MARRIED TO
Addison	11-23-1827	Lucy Reeves (first)
		Amanda Black (second)

William	About 1828	Rebecca Cecil
Nancy	3-1-1829	Sam Edgmon
Jefferson	About 1832	Margaret Keeton
Joel (Joe)	About 1835	Sarah Edgmon
Robert	4-21-1837	Matilda Whitely
Francis (Frank)	About 1839	Josie Basham

Nancy Villines Edgmon, wife of Som Edgmon and only daughter of very early settlers, Hezekiah and Elizabeth Penn Villines.

AGRICULTURAL CENSUS INFORMATION FOR NEWTON COUNTY, ARKANSAS

— June 1, 1860
VALUE OF FARMS $200,000
Number of Horses 1,265
Asses and Mules 129
Milch Cows 1,079
Working Oxen 805
Other Cattle 1,725
Sheep 1,844
Swine 9,804
VALUE OF LIVESTOCK $171,729
Bushels of Wheat 8,716
Bushels of Rye 1,401
Bushels of Indian com 193,157
Bushels of Oats6,050
Pounds of Tobacco 17,452
Bales of ginned cotton (400#each) 6
Pounds of wool 4,958
Bushels of Irish Potatoes3,393
Bushels of Sweet Potatoes3,551
Pounds of Barley 50
Pounds of butter 31,853
Pounds of cheese 63
Tons of Hay 26
Pounds of Flax240
Pounds of Flax Seed 7
Pounds of Maple Sugar 599
Gallons Sorghum Molasses 3,109
Pounds Beeswax 2,073
Pounds of Honey 27,098
Value of Manufacture, homemade $14,843
Value of Animals slaughtered $27,944

In 1850 there were 17, 758 farms in Arkansas In 1860 there was 30,094 farms in Arkansas

1860 — There were eleven slaveholders in Newton County for a total of 24 slaves; Madison County had 82 slaveholders — 296 slaves; Carroll had 84 slaveholders with 330 slaves; Searcy County had 20 slaveholders with 92 slaves and Yell County had 149 slaveholders with 968 slaves

* * ❖ * ❖ * ❖ ❖

Total for Arkansas in 1860 -1,149 slaveholders with 111,115 slaves
Total for Arkansas in 1850 — there were 5,999 slaveholders

Total population NEWTON COUNTY, ARKANSAS 3,369 (free) —559 families
Only one church in Newton County in 1860
2 in Searcy County; 30 in Carroll County and 4 in Madison County.
United States Census for the Year 1840 — Carroll County, Arkansas, Van Buren Township.

The following families represent the first people to enter the upper Buffalo River area. When Newton County was carved out of Carroll County in 1842, this area then became Van Buren Township, Newton County, Arkansas.

HEAD OF HOUSEHOLD

Reeves, William Reeves, John Reeves, Terrell Frazier, Rich Clark, Samuel Austin, David Clark, William Sams, B. C.
Penn, John Villines, Hezikiah
1840
Farmer, David Harp, Sampson Keith, William B. Villines, Abraham Davis, Isham Harp, Samuel Harp, Ichabod Harp, William

THE OLD WAR

The following April, 1861, the Great Civil War began. Many old timers today refer to it as the "Old War." The agricultural south with a population of eight or nine million faced an enemy of twenty million who were rich in tools and manufactured products. For the first two years, Newton and surrounding counties paid little heed as the war had little effect on population. However, in the beginning of the third year, the war was close to their doorsteps and every life was touched.

Mothers urged their children to take small bites of bread and large sups of milk or water. Food and valuables were hidden and family milk cows guarded day and night as consciences quickly gave way to desperation.

Large groups of Confederate guerrilla fighters roamed the hills and valleys and made life miserable for the union sympathizers and their families. The primary task of these partisan rangers was to discourage entry of Union forces and "Mountain Feds" (Union bushwhackers) into Newton County. Because deplorable acts have to be committed in time of war and because of misunderstanding and prejudice, many of these southern patriots were tagged with the stigma of "bushwhacker" or "breshwhacker."

This section of the Ozarks was called the "border" since Missouri, though a southern state, was under federal control and sympathy.

Many Newton County folks still had strong family ties in those northern states which had stayed with the union. They felt that the basic issue of the war was slavery, and their sympathy therefore, stayed with the union, even though Arkansas had seceded. Those who had lived in Arkansas for at least fifteen years were true southerners and the heaviness in their breasts would not let them betray the south. They did not believe that slavery was an issue, but simply that the north was forcing them into a situation which totally disagreed with their strong convictions. Because of their independent natures and the fresh memory of how they had carved a new life for themselves and families in Arkansas, they chose to secede in mind, body and spirit.

It has been estimated that approximately fifty percent of Newton County's population was for the Union and the other fifty percent for the Confederacy. Often, fathers and sons were on opposite sides and brothers divided their sentiments and joined different sides. Family breakups were common and were to stay in feud-like tension for a hundred years thereafter. For them, the war never ended.

Nor was it different for the Villines. There were "up the creek Democrat Villines" and "down the creek Republican Villines." None of the old timers were ever able to divorce themselves from their beliefs that all Democrats were (and are) southerners and all Republicans were (and still are) northerners or unionists. That is how it was, is now and supposedly always will be as long as they live.

Some Villines joined the Union Army and some, the Confederate, while others hid out and joined guerilla bands.

Some switched back and forth and some turned Union toward the end of the war out of sheer desperation and/or frustration.

During the war, Old Abraham, now feeble and senile, lived off the land, dodging bushwhackers. He ate berries in season and fished the Buffalo and roasted his fish over a tiny fire. Independent to the end, he would not live with any of his children or grandchildren after Martha died in 1862. He often slept in caves or wherever night found him. Only during severe weather would he consent to coming into one of their homes.

He must have been terribly confused and discouraged at the war and its resulting deprivation. Then, one day at sundown, as he walked toward the river, he heard horsemen and hurried his ancient legs to hide out but not before some bushwhackers topped the hill. They saw the old man scurrying along and thinking him up to no good or that he had money or food, rushed him and ran a bayonet through him. Some of the Villines womenfolk and Aunt Piety were out looking for old Abraham and found him lying in a pool of blood. They buried him where he lay and covered his frail body with dry leaves, rocks and tears.

Death has claimed all those who knew where he was buried and his gravesite has been lost to another time. Only God knows from where the old patriarch will resurrect.

"Your old men shall dream dreams your young men shall see visions."

— Hosea 2:27

EARLY DAYS IN NEWTON COUNTY

A great-granddaughter of Hezekiah and Elizabeth Villines, Pearlie Villines Mabee of Springfield, Missouri, was most helpful in the research for early activities in Newton County. Some are related here in her own words:

"I am descended from the first Villines to settle in Newton County, Hezekiah and Elizabeth Penn Villines. My grandparents were William and Rebecca Cecil Villines. Part of the old house my grandfather built and where my father was born and raised still stands at Ponca just above the river. My mother told me many things she remembered doing when a girl.

"They would card and spin wool from their own sheep; also from cotton they raised they would spin the thread, then dye it with bark and roots. Walnut hulls would dye brown, also red oak bark dyed brown and hickory bark, a beautiful yellow. Poke berries dyed a purple and there were many others. They would weave the thread into cloth for dresses, men's suits and all their clothes, for that matter. Also, they would knit stockings, gloves and caps.

"Mother said they would butcher a cow or a young yearling in the fall and dry the beef. Candles were made from the tallow or fat from the cow and they would make enough candles to last all winter, for they didn't even have kerosene to burn for light then.

"They also raised and butchered plenty of hogs and cured the hams, bacon and sausage and lard was made for frying and baking.

"They made their own soap; also the lye the soap was made with. They would build what they called an ash hopper made with boards. They put the ashes from the hardwood they burned in the fireplace until the hopper was full and then they would cover it to keep out the rain. When the first warm days of spring came, they would pour many buckets of water over the ashes. The water would soak the lye from the ashes and the lye would rim from a wooden trough at the bottom into buckets. These buckets of lye water were poured into a large wash kettle with any meat scraps that had been saved all winter. With a big wooden paddle, they stirred and boiled and stirred and boiled until the soap was just like they wanted it. They would make enough to fill a large barrel with soft soap, enough to do them a year. This kind of lye won't make a cake. You have to have bought lye for that. It usually took at least three days to make enough soap to last.

"Every homestead had a large orchard of apples, peaches, pears, plums and of course cherries for cherry pie. Fall was a very busy time, canning and drying fruit for the long winters. Mother and her sisters worked in the fields picking cotton. Her mother would clean the house and cook dinner for the large family and put up a quilt. Then, at night after working all day in the field, they would place a candle in the center of the quilt and quilt it out before they went to bed. She said they didn't mind, though, because they sang and told stories or asked riddles and had fun. They also had camp meetings every year which lasted two or three weeks at a time.

"The neighbors would all get together to help each other. If someone needed a house he would cut the logs and haul them to the place he had selected and set a date and invited the neighbors to come help. They would soon have the walls all finished. The women and girls would cook a big dinner and they would all eat and have a good fellowship and if they got the floor finished, they would have a square dance that night.

"They would have spelling bees, quilting parties, music parties, candy breakings and anyone who played an instrument was always welcome at any party. My grandfather, Jim Evans played a violin. He was from the Great Smokey Mountains of Tennessee and came to Arkansas in 1875.

"Folks raised everything they needed except sugar, coffee, salt, soda and a few other items. The coffee came in green berries and had to be roasted in the oven and then ground in a coffee mill, and didn't it smell good! Mother had a wooden box green coffee had come in. Everything that was bought had to be hauled by wagon and team all the way from Springfield, Missouri or Clarksville, Arkansas and both trips took several days.

*Rebecca Cecil Villines,
daughter of Joseph and
Margaret Cecil and wife
of William Villines (he
was son of Hezekiah and
Elizabeth Penn Villines)*

"My father Marion Villines was a very young boy during the Civil War (born 1861) and remembers going over to the Union camp in the field in front of their home. A colored lady cook gave him a piece of fried chicken. This might have been the same colored lady who took Grandmother Villines' lard out of the crock with her hands. Grandmother picked up a heavy shovel and told her if she put her hands in her lard again, she would break her neck. She went on and left the lard alone.

"My Grandfather Villines, Hezekiah, died before the Civil War as a fairly young man, or at least before the slaves were free, because Great Grandmother Villines was left with four slaves, Aunt Piety and her three sons. Piety stayed on with Great Grandmother after she was free and took care of her until her death. Great grandmother and Great Grandfather Villines and the colored lady, Piety, are buried in the Old Hez Villines field between Waymon Villines' home and his parent's home. The colored slave did have a marker. (Note by the author: This last statement is contradicted by some who believe that they are not buried here but rather at Tom Thumb Cemetary and then some say at Gaither and some simply say they do not know.)

"I remember hearing my folks talk about my Great, Great Grandfather Abraham Villines who led the wagon train that came to Arkansas long ago.

During the war, he was old and had gotten so he couldn't remember much and would roam about staying here and there and would catch him fish out of Buffalo River and roast them on a stick over a little fire. It's said the bushwhackers killed him and no one seems to remember where he is buried. But the women helped bury him.

"The picture here of my grandmother, Rebecca Cecil Villines was the only picture of her I have ever seen. I don't know how old she was when the picture was made. She is buried at Beechwood as are most of my people on the Villines side."

"Nostalgia has often been defined as the realization that things weren't as unbearable as they seemed at the time."

— Anonymous

Grave marker of Piety Villines, good and faithful servant of the Villines
for all her life.

. . . AND MORE VILLINES

From Abraham descended multitudes of Villines down to the Frank Villines of this book. But before coming to Frank, there is an interesting and humorous tale about the number of Villines in Newton County.

Many years ago, mail inspectors periodically came through to audit the books and make inquiries relating to the various post offices and the postmasters. At the time of this story, a Mr. Villines was postmaster at Boxley, Arkansas and it came his turn to be "investigated."

The inspector asked everyone he met along his way their names and everyone seemed to be a Villines. Never had he seen a place so completely domiciled by them. He couldn't, he knew, inquire from one of them about the Villines postmaster. He was just about to concede when he saw a big, barefoot, strapping Negro man with his britches rolled up, coming his way grinning from ear to ear. Ah, hah, thought the inspector, now, I shall have my information. He approached the smiling fellow and introduced himself and asked his name.

"Tim Villines," was the proud and happy reply.

The inspector left shaking his head in bewilderment.

Big Tim Villines, the last Negro to live in Newton County, died around the turn of the century. He was one of the children of Piety Villines, the young female slave given to Hezekiah and Elizabeth Villines. It is believed all three of Piety's sons were fathered by a slave over on Little Buffalo by the name of Rowland (might be spelled Roland). Tim, like his mother before him, was given the name Villines as was the custom for slaves.

After the Civil War, most of the Negroes left but Tim and some of his family and mother remained until their deaths. It is believed that some of them moved into Oklahoma. Tim, his wife, Rosetta, and two of his sons, John and Willie, are buried at Beechwood Cemetery near Ponca. Piety and Tim's first wife, Nancy, are buried a short distance away in a family burial plot.

Tim raised two large families and was well thought of for his honesty and integrity. He had a reputation for giving his employers their money's worth for a days' work.

...AND FRANK VILLINES

Abraham was the father of Copeland; Copeland the father of Albert (Ab) and Albert the father of Frank Villines.

Frank was born James Franklin Villines on January 22, 1885 near Low Gap, Newton County, Arkansas. He was the fourth child born to Albert and Rachel Tennessee Minton Villines.

Frank was three years old when his mother died suddenly. The trauma left a deep scar in the sensitive child. His younger sister, Lou, was fortunate to be only eighteen months old — she would forget her mother.

Ab Villines, though young and strong, was heartbroken at the untimely death of his wife. He knew he wouldn't be able to manage with five small children alone. Three months after Rachel's death, he married Jenny Eoff and brought her home to mother his children.

Jenny was just seventeen but had been raised to work and was a natural born manager. The long table groaned with good, nourishing food and all the childrens' clothes were neatly mended, washed and ironed. She was a strong young woman, but under the staggering weight of her new and tremendous responsibility, there was little time for the physical affection of a love-hungry little boy, who missed his mother passionately.

Frank was the only one of the children who didn't love Jenny right away. He couldn't for the life of him, even look at her. He remembered only his mother and no one would take her place.

Frank's obvious dislike for his stepmother concerned Ab Villines after a few years and he often spoke to his son about it. He explained why Frank must respect and help Jenny. Frank loved his father and wanted to please him, so he promised to try and do better. He knew she was good to them all and he did try to be more understanding.

Ab and Jenny had fourteen children of their own, three of whom did not reach their majority; two were stillborn and one died as a young child.
BORN TO AB AND RACHEL
Frank, who first married Pearl Wishon and then Frankie
Henderson Dona, who married Henry Eoff ;Ira, who died in the fall of 1897
Rosie, who married Calvin Eoff Lou, who died in the fall of 1908
BORN TO AB AND JENNY
Delia, who married Jess Thompson
Rosetta, who married Luna Henderson

Martin, who died as a young child
Jim, who married Janie Arbaugh
Nora, who married William A. "Bud" Arbaugh
Albert, who married Louis Barnes
Fred, who married Elsie Warren
Coy, who married Viola Arbaugh
Sara, who married Jim Jackson
    (second time to Charley Villines)
Fay, who married Edgar Barnes
Ray, Fay's twin, who married Arbie Henderson
Bill, who maried Orpha Arbaugh

Because education did not hold the importance it does today, no one encouraged Frank to continue his schooling beyond the third reader. However, he continued reading everything he could find and learning on his own.

Frank's father taught him to work and be proud of a job well done. He showed him how to break the rich earth and turn its damp face to the warm sun; to plant seeds and feel excitement as they burst forth into the light, soon to yield their fruit abundantly.

ALBERT V. VILLINES (Uncle Ab) Father of Frank Villines 1855-1922

ALBERT V. VILLINES AND WIFE, JINCEY EOFF VILLINES (Frank's father
and stepmother)

Frank Villines and sister, Lou
1907

Ab strictly believed that ancient adage, "idle hands are the devil's playhouse," and literally saw that no playhouses were built.

On the rocky hill farm all the children shared in the many tasks. They did the work of grown men and women such as cutting and hauling logs and splitting rails. This was done by girls as well as boys.

There was the hoeing and chopping of cotton, then the picking in the early fall; the harvesting of apples, peaches, pumpkins and corn, all of which were either dried or canned for winter use.

The girls could drive a team of mules and horses as well as any man. But, they also knew how to be feminine and helpless when they wanted to.

There was no need for physical fitness programs nor was there boredom or unhappy children with "hangups". Hard work, sprinkled with laughter and jokes and good eats made the Villines children hardy and handsome as tall cedars.

They worked even while they rested. After supper, the children were each given a pile of cotton to "seed" and only when their piles was finished could they go to bed. Frank, who was a prankster, often slipped some of his cotton into the piles of his unaware sisters and usually went to bed far ahead of the others.

After the com was harvested, the children shelled it by lamp or firelight to be carried to the grist mill and ground into meal for bread.

On days when it was too wet to do other things, each child was given a pouch and pick and sent to hunt "sang" (ginseng). With the proceeds from the "sang" the children could buy things for themselves. The girls would buy a bright piece of material for a new dress or shoes and a pretty hat. The boys a good pocket knife or a box of shells or maybe an extra pair of overalls.

Hardly anyone, adult or child, wore shoes in the warm months and many a stone bruise occupied an innocent foot. But even this painful condition did not give cause for the sufferer to neglect his chores. He just hobbled through them and hoped it would be better tomorrow.

Frank, from his miles of walking the hills, grew strong and muscled. His feet were tough as sandpaper in the summer from walking and scampering over the rocks; his skin was the color of cedar lumber.

He grew in body and mind. The Ozarks held everything he wanted and needed. When he felt alone or misunderstood, he sought the silence and refuge of the hills and the Buffalo River.

You are a human boy, my young friend. A human boy, O glorious to be a
human boy . . .
0 running stream of sparkling joy to be a soaring boy . . .

— Charles Dickens

III

... FROM THE TURN OF
THE CENTURY

. . . And love of Truth, and all That Makes a Man.

— Tennyson

Lou Villines grew into a beautiful young lady and was loved by everyone who knew her. When one is beautiful, lovable and intelligent, it seems they are often fragile.

Frank watched her health wither away and sat by her sick bed nine days and nights with only short naps to refresh him. He held her hand as she gave up her spirit and died September 11, 1908. She was twenty years old. A little piece of Frank died with her.

He grieved for some time, but soon realized that death and its accompanying pains are only temporary, both to the dying and those remaining. And no matter how torn apart you are when a dear one dies, time, the blessed healer, is able to eventually bring you back.

When Lou died, it brought to mind other deaths Frank had known; his dear and beautiful mother and his stalwart brother, Ira, struck down at seventeen by that killer, pneumonia.

Frank now considered himself a man and was usually ready to prove it if the need arose. He loved the Ozarks passionately and could never imagine himself rooted elsewhere but on the Buffalo River.

Until he was old enough to get paying work, he dug ginseng and golden seal roots for cash money. He trudged up and down the hills and through gorges looking for the aromatic herbs.

Frank had courted many girls by the time he was twenty-two, but the only girl who had any real meaning was Pearl Wishon. Pearl was a pretty little thing, who was rather quiet and wore a sad smile. They seemed good for each other and were inevitably paired off at the young folks' gathering.

They were married quietly when Frank was twenty-two and Pearl sixteen. Frank was working in the Cedar Harvest at the time. From the beginning, things seemed to go wrong for Frank and Pearl. They never had a place of their own and this was probably a factor in why things happened as they did.

Frank's work kept them apart and he was able to see her only occasionally at his sister's home where he had secured room and board for her. They were tense and uneasy the whole time they were together.

Frank loved Pearl dearly, but he was a man of strong independence. He had not been schooled on the strange ways of a woman expecting a child, and he received her cool behavior as a hint that she no longer cared for him. He tried every way he knew to get her to smile and be happy. He bought her a good, warm coat which she refused and other things within his financial means. She turned them all down, giving no reason.

Pearl Wishon Villines, Frank's first wife and son, Clyde Villines

Inside she must have screamed for understanding and love, but she too was independent and a hill woman. If he couldn't see her needs, she certainly wouldn't tell him.

And so it went — two stubborn people, making each other miserable without wanting to or knowing why they were doing so.

Frank, disillusionment and youth, his only crimes, placed some money on the mantle board and left. He never saw her again except once at a distance.

Their son, Clyde Villines, was born May 3, 1909 and was twelve years old before Frank saw him. Pearl had married again to a man named Sam Russell and died giving birth to a child when she was twenty-five years old. Sam Russell died three years later and Clyde went to live with a kindly couple by the name of Hofstetter.

Frank desperately wanted his son, but he also had remarried and knew it wouldn't work out under the circumstances. And too, it would have greatly saddened the Hofstetters who loved Clyde as their own.

Until recently, Frank did not know where Pearl was buried. When he found her grave, he reached out and touched the stone. Memories must have flooded his minds as tears came to his eyes. Pearl Wishon Villines Russell is buried at the cemetary just outside Kingston, Arkansas.

— The chain of wedlock is so heavy that it takes two to carry it — sometimes three.

—Anonymous

In 1918 Frank married Frankie Henderson, a pretty school teacher, ten years his junior. Frank considered her "refined" and was proud of her. She added much to his life. But, again, he had married an independent, headstrong woman and theirs was not to be the happy and peaceful life they both wanted.

However, they were able to hang on and each held respect for the other. They were both quiet by nature and worked well together seeming to instantly know the other's mind.

Frank and Frankie had only one daughter, Freeda, but she was enough to flood their lives with sunshine.

Frankie continued teaching school for a number of years after they married. She possessed a dignity Frank could never seem to match. He marveled at the things she knew and complimented her to his friends, but their marriage was strained and quiet.

It remained such until shortly before Frankie's death a decade ago. A great dam seemed to crumble and pent up emotions gushed from them both. All the years of silence and frustration were over. They found each other at last and were inseparable until her death.

Frankie Henderson Villines is buried in the cemetery at Jasper, Arkansas.

Frankie Henderson Villines
and Freeda Villines
(Frank's family)

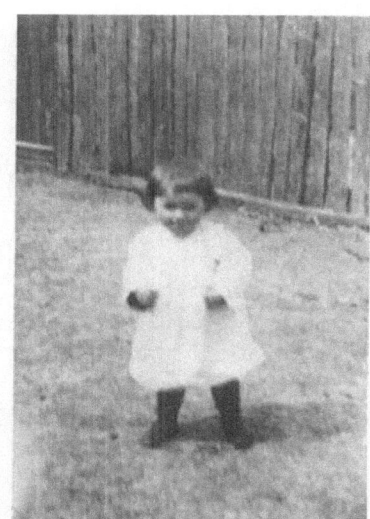

...RECOLLECTIONS

— if any would not work, neither should he eat.
2nd Epistle St. Paul to Thessalonians

Forty Years and
One Bucket of Lard

Frank and Frankie lived on the Buffalo River at the site of what is now known as Kyle's Landing in Township 16 for forty years. During that time, they only *bought* one bucket of lard. There is a story behind this: If you didn't hunt it, trap it, catch it, raise it, swap for it or make it yourself, you just didn't have it when Frank was raising his family. It took hard work and some ingenuity to survive in the rough, yet bountiful hills, and if you weren't made out of good stuff, you either succumbed to the hard life or left it for an easier one.

Frank didn't have to go far from his dooryard to get a "mess" of meat, greens, fish or fur. The entire county was a do-it-yourself supermarket and general store. In exchange for physical exertion and cleverness, one could bring home the bacon or anything else needed or wanted for existence and pleasure.

Wild turkeys were so numerous it was often necessary to stand guard while the hogs ate the corn placed in their pens or the turkeys would eat it all first.

Frank and Frankie and Freeda lived well by the code of EAT IT UP, WEAR IT OUT, MAKE IT DO OR DO WITHOUT for many years.

Of all the products Frank raised, hunted, caught or swapped for, he was most successful with hogs. He and Frankie butchered five or six every year, rendering out the gallons and gallons of snowy white lard. He often swapped lard for items he didn't have since he always made many gallons more than his small family would need.

One day a certain neighbor came to his home lugging a big bucket of freshly picked huckleberries. He wanted to swap them for twelve pounds of lard. This pleased Frankie since she hadn't time to gather any of the luscious huckleberries which literally carpeted the woods around them.

This neighbor was somewhat noted for trying to pull a "fast deal" and Frank knew it. He took the berries in the kitchen and Frankie poured them into a large pan. Underneath were scrawny, mashed and trashy berries, hardly worth keeping. Frank went to the smokehouse and filled an eight pound bucket with lard and carried it back to the yard and gave it to the man. The look on Frank's face told him he had been found out. He took his lard, thanked Frank and was on his way. He later told it around that Frank Villines was the only man he knew who could get twelve pounds of lard into an eight pound bucket.

Frank always fattened or finished his hogs on com to make the lard firm. One year, he had to let them fatten on beechnuts and acoms and this gave the lard a bluish color and not firm.

He smoked the hams, shoulders and bacons with sassafras and hickory wood giving the meat a delicious flavor. He gained a reputation for curing the best meat for miles around.

The meat which couldn't be eaten fresh right away was made into sausage and the fat rendered into lard. The leavings from the lard called "cracklins" were crisp and golden brown and were put aside for snacking and making cracklin' cornbread.

Frank rigged up a platform and scalding vat for slaughtering and dressing (or undressing) the enormous hogs, so the chore wouldn't be so hard. Because of this, he and Frankie could butcher two a day without having to call on the neighbors for help.

Frank once raised a little orphan gilt on a bottle and she made him a fine sow, producing many pigs in each litter. She stayed on the place for many years until she no longer had teeth. For awhile Frank soaked com for her to soften it, but knew he couldn't keep it up as it seemed the old sow was going to live forever. But neither could he bring himself to butcher her because of the tender feeling he had for her. So, he sold her to a neighbor over the way.

On his way to Mt. Sherman one day, he was invited to eat at another neighbor's home where he was served some fine pork steak. Afterwards, he commented on the fine meat and his host told him he had bought it from Mr. So and So, the man to whom Frank had sold the old family sow. Frank thought for a moment he was going to be ill.

To live in one spot for forty years and find it necessary to *buy* only one bucket of lard, and then only because their hogs came down sick and died, proves that Frank and Frankie Villines were industrious people who capitalized on nature and their wits and energy to sustain themselves handsomely.

— The kindly fruits of the earth, so as in due time we may enjoy them —
— The Book of Common Prayer

The house where Frank lived for 40 years. This land and buildings now belong to the National River and it is hoped the house will be restored for interpretive purposes. The house is located between Bear and Indian Creeks on Buffalo River. 1972.

The Walking Larder

"If a man love the labor of his trade, apart from any question of success or fame, the gods have called him.

— Robert Louis Stevenson

Frank Villines was noted for his ability to fish, trap and hunt. In reality, he was good at these things only because of dogged perseverance. It was against his grain to let a fish, a bobcat or a big turkey gobbler outsmart him, and it was a matter of personal challenge, not to mention food for the larder.

One fall morning in the early 1930's, Frankie announced that she'd sure like a mess of squirrel. Frank walked down the Buffalo River to his favorite hunting spot and before long had five big fox squirrels in the poke he swung over his shoulder.

He walked along enjoying being alive on that frosty fall day when he spied a ground hog, which he promptly shot and bagged.

He then came to a creek and there, thick as hair on a dog's back in a little hole of water were a whole passel of fine sucker fish. He took hook and line from his overall pocket and grabbed more than enough for a fine meal and put them in his now heavy poke.

Suddenly, a big flock of ducks rose from the nearby river and Frank downed three with one shot and stuffed them in his bag.

Walking along the edge of the field, he remembered burying two fine watermelons near the woods. He kicked back the dirt and there they were good as when buried. He put one in his poke and the other in the bib of his overalls.

By now, Frank looked like an old peddler all humped over with his wares.

On the way home, he saw a thick vine running into some bushes. He followed it and found two nice pumpkins snug as a bug in a rug. These, he tied together and carried by their vines, like a handle on a valise.

Almost home now, he came upon a neighbor noted for his non-productiveness. The neighbor greeted Frank: "Howdy, Frank, looks like you got enough eatin' to last you'uns all winter."

"Yeah, reckon I got a little."

"I been ahuntin' squirrel all morning and ain't got none yet. The ole woman ain't feelin' so good and cravin' for some squirrel stew."

Frank dug down into his poke and pulled out a big fox squirrel for which his neighbor thanked him again and again.

Later, Frank mentioned the incident to Frankie, who said she'd saddle the mare and go see if there was something she could do for his wife.

As she neared the house, the "ole woman" was sitting on the front porch rocking back and forth and happily greeted Frankie.

Frankie looked past her and saw the "ole man" sitting at the table eating squirrel stew.

Frank said next time, he'd give him the old ground hog.

A severe depression had the nation almost paralyzed at that time, but its sting wasn't particularly felt by Frank and <u>his</u> family. They had never heavily relied on the dollar for their living, nor had most other hill folk.

Anyone "worth his salt" had a good milk cow or milk goats, a few chickens, a brood sow or two and raised their vegetables and a patch of 'lasses cane plus a few fruit trees.

If something was needed and no money on hand, the barter system was used such as Frank did about the lard for the huckleberries. He often traded lard for shoes, meat for grain or flour and molasses for yard goods to be made into clothing. In fact, Frank once exchanged a "ham of meat" for a man's interest in a quarter section of good land. That man was Doc Moore, discussed elsewhere in this book.

Later, during the Second World War when so many things were rationed and hard to come by, Frank and his family continued to live well by their industry and ingenuity.

Frank recalls a time he was invited to go on a big overnight deer hunt and each hunter was required to bring his own "grub."

Frank went to the smokehouse, took his knife and sliced off a quarter of side meat, heavily streaked with lean and cured to perfection with sassafras and hickory wood smoke.

When his fellow hunters began to drag out their own eats, Frank pulled out side meat. Eyes popped and mouths flew open. One man exclaimed: "Good God, Frank I ain't seen that much meat in a month of Sundays. I bet it'd be worth thirty dollars."

Frank grinned and began to share it out. "Remind me to give you fellows lessons sometime on how to raise and cure your own meat."

The Night of the Mad Fox

"Tar-baby ain't saying nuthin', en Brer Fox, he lay low . . ."
— Uncle Remus Tales by Joel Chandler Harris

Foxes were a real nuisance around Frank and Frankie's place on the Buffalo River. No chicken was safe unless roosting high in big cedar trees or safe inside a chicken house. Young pigs were shut up securely for the night. Word had been sent around that rabies was ravaging and many animals bitten by mad foxes had died.

Frank trapped Brother Fox and was very successful. The hides weren't worth the time it took to skin and stretch them, so he just stacked the carcasses in the woods and left them.

Chickens were a very important supplement to the hill people's diet. They furnished eggs and hatched their chicks and multiplied. When the housewife felt they were no longer laying, the big fat ones became chicken and dumplings or chicken and dressing. When they were laying well, the housewife sold the surplus and bought little extras for the house or a piece of cloth off a bright bolt of goods at the Mt. Sherman Store.

Frankie's hens were important to her too. She had some stubborn ones that refused to roost inside the chicken house, but chose a low limb of a big cedar nearby for the nightly abode. She knew about the rabid foxes and listened carefully for any distressful cry from the chicken house or tree roost.

The night was sultry and Frankie couldn't sleep. She tossed and turned and her eyes seemed to get wider with each minute. She heard a hen squawk!

She jumped from her bed, not bothering with shoes, light nor gun. She ran toward the chickens yelling "Shoo", "Git" and other exclamatory remarks of be gone, you varmint!

She saw the outline of an animal about the size of their dog and thought for an instant it was him. Before she had time to call his name, the animal, caught in the act of chicken stealing, lunged. Quick as lightning, she grabbed it by the throat as it bit her ankles over and over again. She lost her balance and fell part way on top of the fox. She could feel its hair, much longer than a dog's, and the snarling, heavy breathing told her it was a fox for sure.

She screamed for Frank, whom she had not awakened. He had been tired from the field work, and she thought she could handle it. But now, she screamed his name over and over as the fox wiggled and squirmed trying to get from under her. She still held fast to his throat.

Frank leaped from the bed at the sound of his name, grabbed a pistol he kept near his bed and ran to his wife. Frankie saw the gun and cried, "Don't shoot him, Frank, you might hit me!"

He quickly took in the situation and tried to reassure her.

"Frankie, hold his head out aways from you and be still. I'll not hit you, don't worry."

She eyed her husband and knew he was an excellent shot and this close, he wouldn't miss. She eased the nearly limp fox's head out from her as far as she could, closed her eyes and Frank fired, killing him instantly.

Frankie let him drop to the ground as Frank helped her to her feet.

"He bit me, Frank, he bit me lots of times." He helped her to the kitchen where he lighted a lamp and washed her wounds.

He said calmly, "We'd better cut off his head and take it to Mt. Sherman and get someone to take it to Little Rock for tests."

She felt better now that Frank had taken over and nodded her approval, while the chickens squawked their excited relief.

They carried the head to Mount Sherman in a paper bag. It seemed to take forever to hear from Little Rock, but finally the bad news came. The fox was rabid, though only in the first stages, and Frankie had to be subjected to the tortuous series of rabies shots.

But she didn't complain then or ever about anything. She was made of the kind of material that does not whine — she was a mountain woman.

Afterwards, Frank declared war on every fox in Newton County. That year, he killed twenty-five. Soon, the fox, as in the Tales of Uncle Remus, "he lay low."

"Many foxes grow gray, but few grow good."

— Benjamin Franklin

Leness House and Burt Hamilton (Just before World War I days)

Who's Afraid of the Big Bad Bees

And now the matchless deed's achieved, Determined, Dared and Done.
— Anonymous

    Leness House and Burt Hamilton trudged along the dusty road on their way to the creek to catch a mess of linesides for supper. Up ahead a small crowd had gathered at Bee Bluff where crude sycamore ladders had been constructed and leaned in rickety fashion against the high limestone bluff.
    The curious young men approached the noisy crowd to gee what was going on. Several men had decided to rob the bee hive high above in the

side of the bluff, (so named for this reason) which they knew to be full of honey.

Years earlier it had been robbed and many pounds of honey taken out. Those earlier robbers had come over the top of the bluff and descended on ropes and removed what they could, but the job was far from complete.

Leness and Burt eyed the rickety, makeshift ladders. The wives of some of the adventurous souls were wildly objecting to their men embarking on such a fool hardly excursion. Each time one of them climbed a few feet off the ground, some bonneted female with hands on hips shrieked for him to come down immediately.

Leness and Burt, not having any female objectors, and being young with devil-may-care hearts, offered their services to rob the hive for half the honey. After a little discussion, it was agreed. By now, the festive spectators had increased in number.

At that time in 1916 Ponca was a thriving mining community and little shacks and tents dotted every accessible spot around.

That night, the two lean and lank young fellows climbed the crude ladder armed with sulphur rags and clay mud. They crammed the rags into a small opening some hundred and twenty-five feet up the side of the bluff, lighted them, stopped up the hole with the clay mud and came down.

Early next morning the two scooted up the ladder as though they did it every morning before breakfast; this time to inspect the condition of the bees. Sure enough, all were dead and no sound came from within.

Inside they could see honey galore for at least six feet back into the opening. They reached all they could, but the opening was entirely too small to have room to work.

Not to be outdone before an audience of some three hundred people below, they went down and got dynamite, hammer and a piece of steel. They drilled a six inch hole and placed two inches of "giant powder" inside. Then they attached a fuse, lighted it and backed a safe distance down the ladder. The small explosion gave them room to work, but still they couldn't reach far enough back into the inky blackness to really "get with it."

Down the ladder once more and to the blacksmith shop in Ponca where they had Mr. Dick Sparks construct a long honey knife. The "smith" took a six foot piece of rod iron and made a sharp knife on one end and a hook on the other. They would enable them to cut through the thick comb, hook it and bring it to the front of the hive.

The knife worked well, but even so, their progress was slow. They sent water bucket after water bucket filled with golden honey and comb down ropes to the waiting crowd, assured that at least every other bucket was being reserved for them.

Late that afternoon, two tired young men sent the last bucket of honey down the rope and went down. They knew much honey had been eaten, but were taken aback with surprise to learn that the sweet-hungry crowd had consumed all but one eight pound bucket. Everyone congratulated them and slapped them on the back for a job well done. They looked at each other and took the little bucket of honey and walked on down the road. Not much reward for the amount of work. A little ole' bucket full and all their clothes, hair and skin would hold.

Suddenly, they stopped their grumbling and started laughing at the irony of it all. They slapped each other on the back. What'd they care. They had enough honey to eat and everybody for once had had a dog's bait of honey, probably for the first time in their lives. That made them feel better, plus the fact that they were sort of heros for the day in the eyes of that crowd. They headed for the creek to wash off the sticky and then get on with the business of catching a mess of fish for supper. That's what they'd set out to do the day before anyway.

— The action is best, which procures the greatest happiness for the greatest number —

— Francis Hutcheson

Christmas in Newton County

Heap on more wood! — the wind is chill;
But let it whistle as it will
We'll keep our Christmas merry still.

— Sir Walter Scott

Around the first of December, it was the custom for Abner Villines, Frank's father, and a couple of his neighbors to load their wagons with apples, pumpkins and any other marketable items and head for Springfield, Missouri to barter and get supplies for Christmas and the needed items for the coming year.

The trip took a week or more depending on the unpredictable weather. It was an exciting time indeed when the wagons returned loaded down with barrels, casks, sacks and mysterious looking boxes. One hundred Fifty pound barrel of salt was generally bought on the Christmas trip in December. The salt cost $1.50 and lasted the family for about a year. It was used for curing meat, for the livestock and human consumption.

Things that weren't raised or made were also purchased. There were new shoes (one pair a year), bright bolts of gingham and spools of thread, hard candy and oranges.

In the Villines household, many cakes were baked on the big iron stove several weeks before Christmas. Molasses was the primary sweetener and gave all those goodies a dark, delicious flavor which improved with age.

One December trip, Frank's father brought back a new Springfield wagon. The day of his return to Low Gap was icy cold and bright. The already beautiful new wheels of the wagon were made even lovelier to the young Frank because they were entirely enveloped in ice on that wintry day. They glistened like tinsel on a Christmas tree, only more so.

Gifts, for the most part, were homemade. Highly appreciated was that new gingham dress, bonnet or those knitted warm socks, mittens and caps. Often, the boys' stockings held a new pocket knife, a most treasured and useful gift.

Frank Villines & Leness House 1913

The long table on Christmas Day sported a huge turkey gobbler baked to perfection with long pans of cornbread dressing, a fresh baked ham and "new" sausage. Baked sweet potatoes held a place of honor along with other vegetables from the cellar, not to mention those delicious pumpkin pies.

All the little Villines children sitting on the long benches around the bountifully filled table, had eyes as shiny as new dimes while they waited for their father to say grace before they dived into the good Christmas dinner.

There were many times when money was rare but never in Frank's life does he remember food being scarce at his table. It certainly could have been, Frank knew, if everyone from the oldest down to the youngest, had not worked hard, long hours to raise it, harvest it and prepare it,

There were some landowners in the county who were healthy, yet never seemed to have the necessities of life. These people were (and are) looked down on by the more industrious ones.

A good living was there but had to be hustled out of the hills where everything had been made plentiful by a benevolent Creator.

Damon and Pythias

Friendship is love without its wings . . .

— Byron —

Frank Villines and Leness House have been arm-around- the-shoulder-pals from their modest beginnings, and are very much like those two unforgettable friends of long ago ...

Many centuries ago, there were two very good friends, Damon and Pythias. According to Roman legend, Pythias was condemned to death because he opposed Dionyouis, the tyrant of Sicily. Pythias begged to be allowed to return home to say goodbye to his wife and child and to place his affairs in order. Damon came forward and offered himself as security for his friend. He said he would die in Pythias' place if for some reason he failed to return. The time for the execution approached and Pythias had not come. Damon stood bravely at the place where he was to die. Pythias suddenly rushed through the crowd into Damon's arms.

Pythias' horse had been killed and it was with great effort that he was able to arrive on time. Then each friend pleaded to die for the other.

Dionyouis was so moved that he pardoned them both and begged to share in their friendship.

The Knights of Pythias, a fraternal society founded in 1864 took its name from the Pythias in this story.

Frank and Leness' friendship began as children when they played together at school. Their bond of friendship was strengthened by the fact that both had lost a parent while very young.

Ruben Leness House was the son of Marion "Dock" House and Cynthia Ann Kilgore House. He was born July 8, 1891 near Low Gap just over the mountain from where Frank was bom.

Frank was a few years older than Leness and helped him get work at the stave mill where he was working. They worked together in the lead and zinc mines at Ponca for two years. The work was hard and the hours long, but both men were conditioned to it and knew no other way of life. Even after ten hours in the mines, they were never too tired to get their poles and head for the creek to get a mess of fresh fish for supper.

Frank and Len, along with some of the other Low Gap boys, had a reputation for being tough. This was probably because of their disciplined bodies, good coarse food and hard work. None of them had ever been known to turn his back on trouble. They rather enjoyed the reputation, but were aware that the toughest things about them were the calluses on their work-worn hands.

In 1918 Len went to World War I, leaving behind his pretty wife, Martha, and their baby daughter, Mildred.

This young, easy going hill man, who had never been far from the Arkansas Ozark Mountains went unquestionably to battle for his country in a strange, distant land for a cause he didn't fully understand. But he felt it was the right thing for him to do, and so he did it.

Another dear friend, Burt Hamilton, who left the hills with Leness and from whom he had never been separated since leaving, was killed just yards from where Len lay in a bloody ditch facing gas and gun with shrapnel in his own leg.

Just days before his discharge, Len contracted spinal meningitis. There was no known cure, but the dedicated army doctors fought desperately for Len's life. Len's determination to live and get back to Martha and the baby were highly instrumental in winning the battle for his life.

Frank was called to the war, but armistice was signed before he received his orders.

After the war, Frank and Len once more began to pal around. Both were married and busy raising their families, but still took time for a relaxing hunting or fishing trip.

One cold day, they went bobcat hunting and had a bottle along to warm them. Neither intended to drink too much but it slipped up on them. As they walked along a gorge singing and enjoying being alive, a silly argument arose and they fought tooth and nail. Len whipped Frank.

They made up and went down the gorge further, once again singing. Suddenly, they stopped and Frank told Len it was just plain luck that he whipped him and another fight began. This time Frank whipped Len. Now, they felt better, each having been victorious. They found a shelter under an overhanging rock and slept it off.

When times were good, they enjoyed them and laughed easily and often. When they were not so good, they took them in their strides but still laughed easily and often. It was a way of life and the only one they knew. It was an unwritten code of the <u>hills</u>: Enjoy prosperity and tolerate hard times and WORK. They had been taught, Len, by a courageous and kind-hearted mother, and Frank, by a stem, work- loving father, that work, honor and security had the same meaning.

In the twilight of his life, Len lost both legs as a result of diabetes and more recently, had to have four fingers amputated from one hand. But nonetheless, he was as cheerful as a mockingbird.

Two years ago, I had the privilege of taking Len (age 85) and Frank (age 90) on a jeep trip down along the Buffalo River. We packed a lunch and a thermos of coffee and bonnced over some of the roughest terrain I had ever seen. We laughed until tears rolled about things that happened at certain spots along our way, called to mind by Frank or Len. Their laughter swelled my heart with gladness and it was a day I shall never forget.

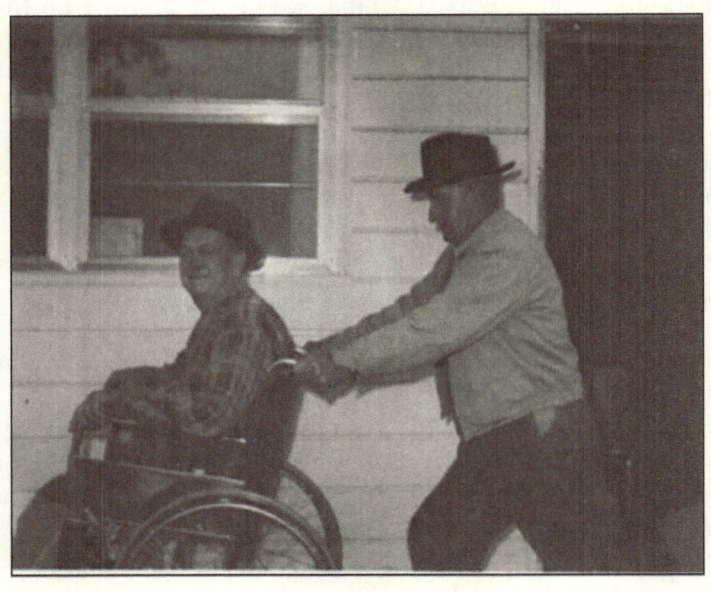

Leness House and Frank Villines
"A friend in need is a friend in deed." 1972

Today, houses along Buffalo are rare, but I was told by Frank and Len that in their day, houses were "ever so often" along the river. They pointed out dense woods that were once large fields of com or other grain.

I thought later of what could have happened if one of them had gotten sick while we were deep down in those hollows. As luck (or fate) would have it, when we pulled into Len's yard, one of the tires went flat. Everyone on the place tried to change that tire, but the lugs were frozen and we finally had to have a service station attendant come out to change it with power tools. A close call.

Both of them thanked me over and over for that trip and each declared that it would probably be the last one for them, and that they would never again be able to see ole Buffalo from the vantage points seen that day. I am far richer for having taken them.

One could listen for hours as these two old fellows talked of days gone by; this twentieth century Damon and Pythias.

Rosie Keith (daughter of Bill Keith) and wife of Burt Hamilton.

It was, in fact, Len's last trip down Buffalo. On September 6, 1977, he passed away. Frank is deeply hurt by his passing as are we all. He told me in a wavering voice that he had "lost his sidekick" and mentioned that sixty-five years ago that month, he had helped Len get on at that stave mill, which was the beginning of a lifelong friendship.

Len was buried from the little white church at Beech- wood and laid to rest in the adjoining cemetery. The church would not hold all the mourners and many stood outside trying to hear the kind words of the preacher and some of the heartwarming comments by one of Len's grandsons.

His many friends of all walks of life, some in fine suits and others in clean overalls, passed by for a last look before the coffin was closed forever and the American flag folded and handed to Martha, his widow.

"Man is the measure of all things."

— Protagoras

'Lasses Makin'

When Frank was growing up in Newton County, molasses was a very important part of the hill people's diet. The size of a family determined how much 'lasses would be needed to see them through. The amount made or bought was never really enough, but with plenty of wild honey and a little maple sugar, a body could make out for sweets.

Ab Villines bought the first metal sorghum mill in Newton County in 1893. The heavy mill was made in Chattanooga, Tennessee and was to squeeze many thousands of gallons of cane juice before it was put to rest.

He hauled the mill by wagon and mules to the various farms. The long, slender cane had been stripped and placed in huge piles to await the arrival of Ab and bis sturdy little mill.

Molasses making in Newton County has always been quite a ritual. The weather needs to be crisp and dry, if possible. The humidity has a lot to do with successful molasses making. Folks gathered at the cook off like they did at a Fourth of July picnic. The festive atmosphere made it an exciting event and a good time to get in some visiting.

Frank's first experience with molasses making was at a very early age. He was about six or eight years old when he first remembers going with his father to make molasses for folks. It was well into November and winter had already made itself known in the hills. Frank's dad told him he could feed the stalks into the mill if he wanted to. This delighted Frank and he began feeding cane and watching the old mule walk slowly around and around supplying the power to squeeze out the liquid. Frank soon was so cold he began to cry and that ended his cane feeding for the day, but he still enjoyed the goings on after he had warmed up.

The good rich smell of the 'lasses cooking in huge pans tickled his nose and made his mouth water. He stood near to watch the men and women taking turns stirring the golden, bubbly liquid, and also it was warm there.

Dry cedar wood was continuously fed the fire underneath the pans which kept the heating consistency just right and the molasses at a rolling boil.

As the 'lasses became "ready" (and it takes a veteran molasses maker to know when), it was poured into waiting buckets. Those who didn't have their own cane could buy molasses from Ab Villines for twenty cents a gallon. Every fall meant many gallons of 'lasses for the Villines Family. When the sixty gallon family barrel was filled, the surplus would be sold.

That family barrel was kept in the comer of the smoke house. When 'lasses was needed in the house, one of the youngsters would take a pitcher and draw it full. One winter evening, someone failed to replace the stopper. Next morning 'lasses had run all the way across the big yard and the hens stuck in it as they attempted to cross the sticky river. Needless to say, somebody got into trouble.

Today, in Newton County, there are still a few 'lasses mills in operation. However, not many people raise their cane today and because of this, permanent mills are set up and folks who do have cane bring it to the mill. Molasses can be bought today for near $10 a gallon. Quite a jump from twenty cents at the turn of the century.

Until recently, Ross Villiness, a cousin to Frank, still made molasses. He really knows his business and people from far and near would place orders months ahead of cook off time for Ross to make 'lasses for them.

Frank remembers with a chuckle when he was in his early teens and very shy about girls, he and his father were making 'lasses at this place and night caught them. The only place for Frank to sleep was with a middle aged lady and apparently, no one thought anything of it except Frank.

The lady blew out the lamp and got into bed, and was soon snoring away. Poor Frank was still debating on how he would handle this uncomfortable situation. His overalls were stiff with molasses, even the buckles, and he could not pull them off as he had nothing underneath that was any less sticky. He wouldn't have pulled those overalls off no matter what he had under them anyway. He lay down on the very edge of the bed and held on.

By now the lady was really "sawing logs" with her snoring and Frank slid off the bed, crept out the door and headed for the creek bank where he planned to sleep. A whole yard full of dogs began barking and running toward him. He yelled at them to hush and all the noise brought his father to the scene.

Frank doesn't remember what story he told his dad, but he does remember he had to go back and sleep on the edge of that bed still wearing his stiff-with 'lasses overalls.

— It was fun to be a boy when all you had to be was good — not superior.

— Anonymous

IV

... AND THERE ARE PEOPLE

Some of Newton County's Early Medical Men

"If I can any way contribute to the diversion or improvement of the country in which I live, I shall leave it, when I am summoned out of it, with the secret satisfaction of thinking that I have not lived in vain."
— Joseph Addison

When the county was young, doctoring often consisted solely of brewing up herbs into teas, balms and salves and pouring it down or rubbing it on the ailing victim. For the lack of anything better, experimentation was the rule and many died from the treatment alone. The cemeteries are filled with the young who died from conditions which today would be considered not serious at all.

Diarrhea, then called "bloody flux", killed many children and hemorrhage at childbirth was too frequent. Appendicitis killed many, as well as flu and pneumonia and food poisoning, all of which could be treated effectively today.

Doctors and dentists with medical degrees were few and far between. There were grannies, however, who could deliver babies as professionally as the best doctor of the day, and herb doctors who could brew up a tea that would knock your hat off and cure the cramps in less than ten minutes and put the sufferer to sleep. Roots and other concoctions were used to stop bleeding and sewing up a wound with regular sewing needle and thread was done frequently. Frank Villines tells of sewing up his own knee after it was laid open by an axe, using regular needle and thread. He used a special green salve on it and in no time at all, only a thin scar remained. When asked if it hurt, he said, "God amighty, yeah, but t'weren't nothin' else to do." Only the fittest survived.

Very little is recorded on the medical men in Newton County before the Civil War, but several have listed since that period and around the turn of the century who have left their mark. Tales and legends are still told about them and their dedicated services to the people of Newton County. Most of them had no diplomas from medical schools, but were highly respected and trusted by the citizens as the "best there is" and the following is an incomplete collection of stories on a few of those dedicated folks, some of whom are still living.

BEAVER JIM

"Beaver Jim" Villines was born James A. Villines in 1854 in Arkansas to the union of William (son of Hezekiah) and Rebecca Cecil Villines. Though just a tyke during the "Old War", he was to have many unpleasant memories about it.

Jim earned his nickname, according to handed down stories, by his ability to trap the beaver. It seems some old fellow gave him a secret bait and because of it, Newton County was dangerous territory for all the little amphibious animals with webbed hind feet and flat tail.

There is another story, less likely, as to why he was called Beaver Jim. One Sunday after church a pretty young lady invited Jim home for dinner with her. Jim was painfully shy and couldn't think of a thing to say on their way home. They came to a cane break and Jim saw where the beaver had been working on the cane and he asked, "Did you see that beaver sign?" She looked as though she couldn't care less and replied, "No, and I ain't looking for any." Word got back to his friends and they called him Beaver Jim from then on.

The truth of the matter was that Jim could trap anything and did. He was a man of great strength and intestinal fortitude. Folks learned quickly that he was a man who could do what had to be done without wincing. He hated to see anyone suffer and went out of his way to help his neighbors. He never charged a fee for any of his services. He lanced their boils, sewed up their wounds and pulled their teeth.

Frank recalls, as a young boy, how a tooth had been bothering him off and on and his father told him he ought to go have it pulled. Frank, fearful down to his toes of just the very thought of it, used every excuse for not going. One day, while he and his father were about to pass Jim's place, the tooth kicked up a fit again and began its miserable throbbing. This time Ab Villines was firm. "Get out, Frank, and go let Jim pull that tooth and don't come home until he does." No sooner had the wagon gotten out of sight, and while Frank climbed the hill to Beaver Jim's place, his tooth stopped hurting. But he remembered his father's words and went on and Jim pulled the trembling Frank's tooth.

Beaver Jim married Sarah Arbaugh, daughter of "Coon" (Conrad) Arbaugh and Fanny Black Arbaugh. They had three children, Ivy, James, Fanny and William, fondly called Billy Beaver after his father.

Jim and Sarah Villines are buried in the far right hand corner at Beechwood Cemetery, in Newton County.

Frank remembers a boat which Beaver Jim built with a foot adz. (an adz is a tool which looks like a grubbing hoe, the cutting edge being at right angles to the handle). He cut a big ash tree to make his boat because ash is good and solid and the sun doesn't seem to crack it over the years, as happens with other wood. He dressed the boat down with a broad axe to about two inches on the side but thicker at the bottom which tapered, making it lighter on top. He bored a hole in the end and tied a rope in it. The boat was about 14 feet long.

Of all the times Old Buffalo went on a rampage, Beaver Jim never let his "dugout" get away. Frank said he used it for maybe twenty years. He fished and trapped with it and hauled people across the river in it since there was no "Low Water" bridge below Ponca then.

Frank says he used Beaver Jim's boat many times and he didn't mind. He said there were many on Buffalo who had such dugouts, but none withstood Buffalo's "fits" like Beaver Jim's did.

DOC MOORE

Beautiful young people are accidents of nature, but beautiful old people are works of art.

— Greenbie

Doc Moore, nearing 90, is still mentally alert, has a keen sense of humor and if he had both legs, would probably be pulling and filling teeth in Newton County just as he has done since May of 1912.

Doc (Dr. 0. A. Moore) was one of five children born to Willis Wilson and Margaret Thompson Moore. He was bom three miles from Dogpatch, Arkansas (then called Wilcock- son community).

His father was a banker and gave his children all the advantages for a good education. Doc started out to study law but later thought dentistry might be a "pretty good racket" (his own words) so he switched over.

He was a true horse and buggy dentist and carried his equipment with him to various communities and set up shop on someone's shady front porch. Through word of mouth, patients came, glassy eyed with pain to have teeth extracted. Doc used a foot engine machine. There was sort of a cable from the top to where a hand piece held a drill. One pedal commanded the use of the foot while the hands were left free to hold the drill (and the patient).

It was quite some time before he convinced people to try and save their teeth by filling rather than extracting. According to them, the quickest way to ease the pain, was to yank 'er out. He wanted to educate his patients to save their teeth and offered to fix a young man's teeth free to prove how much better it would be. He filled almost every tooth in his head and they lasted forty years. The teeth he did not fill had long since been pulled.

According to Doc, he finally convinced some and he charged fifty cents to fill a tooth and twenty-five to extract —never over a dollar in all the fifty years of working with people's teeth. He charged three dollars to fill teeth with gold. He used pure gold, heated it and beat it layer after layer into the cavity.

He recalls many a night of getting up to treat patients. He said the first three years he was a dentist he made just enough for room and board, but then business picked up. Many times, patients didn't have cash and would pay him "in kind" as they did the doctors of the day.

Doc also taught school for a year or so in 1907 and 1908 at Ryker, a community in the extreme northwest comer of Newton County. In 1909 he attended Vanderbilt University for three years in Tennessee and began his practice in dentistry in May of 1912.

Doc's grandfather, John Wilbom Moore homesteaded the site where he was born east of Marble City (Dogpatch) and later moved near Gaither. This grandfather was from Pennsylvania but had his beginnings on the River Rhine in Germany and lived for periods in the Carolinas, Tennessee and then to Arkansas.

Doc married late in life but had no children.

Recalling some of the humorous happenings of his career, he told of a woman at Cave Creek watching him work and she related that the doc was getting ready to put medicine in the "ghooms" (meaning gums).

Another fellow came to him in severe pain and said, "Doc, these old stump teeth are resulting in bad mastication of my food and rearrangement in my stomach."

He said that only during the last ten years or so of his career did he make false teeth and the prices began at $20 and ran as high as $90. Many folks are still wearing teeth which he made for them.

Doc was in World War I but spent his time at Camp Pike and saw no overseas duty.

According to many, Doc has done so much to alleviate pain among thousands and everyone has high praise for him.

He was a civic minded business man and acquired a considerable amount of property. He is the one who swapped Frank Villines forty acres of land for two hams of meat, which land Frank later sold for $600.00. It's certainly a fact that all his business ventures were not of this nature.

Doc had to have one of his legs amputated some time ago but that has not caused him one iota of bitterness. He still speaks softly with a hint of a joke in his voice. He spends his time in Jasper and the nursing home in Harrison where he goes for periodic treatment for his condition. He thoroughly enjoys visitors and a good competitive game of dominoes.

He told me that much of his youth was spent raising cane and drinking too much, but all that was behind him now and according to him, his attitude has changed completely. He believes "if you live by the laws of creation and God, you live longer and better."

* * ❖ * ❖ * ❖ ❖

Before publication of this edition, Doc Moore passed away on July 11, 1977 at the age of 89 years. We should not grieve for this man since "by living according to the laws of creation and God, he lived long and well", and surely, he has a high stool in heaven.

DR. BRANNON

Foster Fillingham and his sister, Mae Maples, two natives of Newton County had the following to say in their article entitled, REMINISCENCES OF THE UPPER BIG BUFFALO RIVER VALLEY:

"We think no one man touched the lives of so many, or had so much influence on them as Dr. Brannon had on the people of upper Buffalo river valley, nor one to whom they are more indebted. He was a middle aged man when we first knew him. It was easy to see he was used to many things that were not to be had on Buffalo, but he always made everybody feel at ease. He was always well-dressed and considerate and when anyone was in need, he was always there. There were rumors of why he was on Buffalo, but I do not know if any of them were based on fact. He would go away and be gone for a time, then come back. If he ever told where he had been, we never heard of it. Father said he told him that his home was in Georgia and that he left there when he was in medical school, when he became involved in some trouble over his sister."

"Dr. Brannon had no regular office. Sometimes he would be at Jimmie Villines, sometimes at the home of Sam Duty, sometimes at Father's home. I am sure he never did have a degree in medicine — he never did say he did — but he had studied medicine. I remember one time when he was staying at our home, father told me to get his sweet tobacco. I went and got it and before I took it to him, I cut myself a generous chew, and went out in the chimney comer to chew it. For awhile it tasted all right, but pretty soon it was not so good, and I looked up at tbe top of the chimney, and it was going around in circles. I jumped up to get out of the way and passed out. Dr. Brannon and my Father found me and carried me in and worked with me about all night."

"Later, Dr. Brannon bought the McKinney Place, out on the mountain near George Beavers, in partners with a man named Harve Bartell. Later Bartell left suddenly and we never heard of him again, nor do we know much of the later years of Dr. Brannon's life. But I saw his grave in Walnut Grove Cemetery."

DOC SOUTHERLIN

After the turn of the century another doctor took up residence in Newton County and settled in at Ponca, much to the relief of the folks there.

Doc was "one of the best "to hear the ole timers tell it and delivered many a baby and did difficult surgery by the light of a coal oil lamp.

He was loved by all. He was a young, single man when he came to Ponca but this was taken care of right away. He was treating a family near Key's Gap for the fever and one of the daughters, Rosie was very beautiful. Her widowed mother could not pay Doc's bill for his many hours of service and he smiled his big handsome smile and said, "I'll settle for Rosie." Rosie returned his smile so willing was her young heart for the big, fine looking doctor.

The doc and Rosie had four children and she died young. Her death almost drove him crazy. He married again later in life.

There was a story that Doc Southerlin came to the hills of Newton County to get away from a lot of bad memories, but no one seems to remember what they were and it's just as well.

Newton County has had its share of good, qualified medical men and this list includes only a few of the old time doctors who had many patients living miles apart with only a horse or buggy rig between them. There were many more but for lack of folks now living to remind me of them, they must be omitted.

Frank Villines tells an incident of many years ago involving a fine man of medicine known as "Ole Doc Kirby." Naturally, he was not old at the time. It seems that the former sheriff of Newton County, Bill Green had a plow handle to bounce off and hit him in the side and the place abcessed and Ole Doc Kirby was sent for (he was living in Harrison at the time). The doctor rode over there which was some 35 miles from his home, on horseback fording streams and the Buffalo River. He put Mr. Green on the kitchen table, removed a section of his rib cage, inserted a tube inside to drain the infected area and the doctor stayed there until he was completely out of danger. When Mr. Green asked him later for his bill, it was only $100. This was for riding 70 miles round trip on horseback, staying several days treating his patient, the surgery and all. Mr. Green was glad to pay it, but many thought that it was a terribly high bill for that day and time. A descendent of Doctor Kirby is presently a practicing physician in Harrison today.

Another form of doctoring was done in Newton County during the period of this book and it was done by bold, strong women called "Grannie Women." These stalwart souls were able to deliver babies, sew up a wound and some could even pull teeth. They were important citizens in the community and respected and loved by everyone.

The following list of "Grannie Women" is by no means complete and it is hoped that the descendents of these very special women will be "made proud" by these few words of praise.

SOME "GRANNIE" WOMEN

AUNT ORLENA CLARK

Aunt Orlena Clark (born Orlena Newberry, daughter of James M. and Rachel Newberry) was the wife of Samuel H. Clark (son of Abraham H. and Sabra Ann Edgmon Clark) and was one of the noted "grannie women" of long, long ago. In time of sickness or need, Aunt Orlena was always there and if mothers didn't know what to do for their sick children, they would always send for Aunt Orlena. Although she had a houseful of children of her own, she was never too busy to come when called. She and her large family lived on the Clark Homestead at Beechwood.

GRANNIE WISHON

Ike Wishon's wife, Cynthia, was a grannie woman in and around the Low Gap community and many a little 'un she helped bring into the world. Frank Villines recalls that she was "stout made", and always pleasant. All the children loved her and would gang up at her house to play. She loved children and made each one feel like she liked them best.

She and her husband Issac Coonrod Wishon are buried at Low Gap.

GRANNIE EVANS

Mollie Fultz Evans, wife of George Evans, was a "grannie woman." Not only was she skilled in birthing babies, but could do almost anything a doctor could do, and often did. She went with the doctors on house calls, namely, Dr. Winnfield Poyner, Dr. Erton Poyner and Dr. Henry Southerland. Mollie was a good sized woman with strong, gentle hands. Most all the women in her family had been midwives and she followed in their footsteps.

Dr. Winnfield Poyner, a very sensitive man, became so involved with caring for his patients, that he cried when one died.

One of Mollie and George's daughters, Mrs. Gertie Evans Studyvin, lives at Compton and is loved and respected by everyone who knows her. She is in her eighties but still active in her church work and uses her telephone to inquire about the sick folks in the community.

She reflected that when she was growing up, their home was always open to travellers. Cattle and timber buyers would take their meals and spend the night at the Evans home.

One of Gertie's sisters, Amo, courted Frank Villines when they were young. Frank tells that she was a very pretty woman and everyone thought they would marry, but he claims that he "fooled around and let somebody else grab her."

George Evans Family

AUNT LIZZIE BRISCO

Aunt Lizzie Brisco, who was known as "The Doctor," lived at Tom Thumb Spring in the Gaither Cove of Newton County. It was often necessary for her to climb through the "Needles Eye" in the cove to hurry to the top of Gaither Mountain to her patients. Needles Eye is so named as it is an opening only large enough for a person to climb through on a ladder. Aunt Lizzie would tie her horse at the foot of the ladder, climb through and someone would be waiting on the other side with another horse to complete the trip to the ailing person.

In some places in the cove the way was so narrow, she would get down and lead her horse through. There were many who thought she was as good a medical doctor as any who had finished medical school.

There are probably many more midwives who cannot be remembered. Frank said there was a Rebecca Potter Beaver who was a "real dandy" of a "grannie".

Some of the "New Breed" discussed elsewhere are becoming aware of natural childbirth and childbirth without medical help. They are learning techniques and teaching each other so that who knows, "grannie women" might be on their way back in Newton County.

"The vocation of every man and woman is to serve other people."
— Leo Tolstoy

MARTHA

For she's the pink of womankind, and blooms without a peer . ...
Robert Burns

Tommy Baker was bom in England. When he was three years old, his parents brought him to America and settled in Kansas. Tommy's father was quite a speculator and made good in the coal mines in Kansas. Later, he came to Newton County where he speculated in land. At his death, he willed all his holdings in Newton County to Tommy, who seemed to be so fond of the area, where he often visited with his father.

Tommy Baker, now grown, handsome and full of life and a need to expand and do well, came to Newton County to be near his land interests of several hundred acres. For a time, he roomed at the home of Addison and Amasida Villines, whom everyone called Uncle Ad and Aunt Mandy. They built the first house in Ponca and raised a large family there, but Tommy had eyes only for their little Susie Villines, a petite young lady of ninety pounds.

After a long courtship, they married quietly and Tommy built them a house overlooking the village of Ponca. To this union, one child was born, namely, Martha Baker, bom July 2, 1901. Another child was bom to them, but did not live.

Tommy and Susie could have given Martha everything her heart desired, but they did not. Instead, they taught her about love, compassion, tenderness and understanding, which went along with her naturally sensitive nature. She was sheltered from all turmoil for as long as possible.

When she was sixteen, she began to notice one of the Low Gap boys, Leness House, who came to her house with Frank Villines, her cousin, to join in one of her father's regular Saturday night dances. Tommy Baker was known far and wide for those dances and suppers. Music from a "banger" and fiddle could be heard ringing throughout the hills on many a Saturday night.

Tommy Baker didn't have much use for the Low Gap boys since their reputation was not so good. He did everything possible to keep Martha from becoming entangled, but all was in vain. Martha Baker had set her cap for the tall, lanky Leness House with an easy smile, whose eyes twinkled with mischief and whose hearty laughter caused her own heart to swell with love. Leness felt the same about the young beauty with the soft skin and innocent, sparkling eyes.

Leness House and bride,
Martha Baker House about 1917

He enlisted the help of Frank to help him get to see her. They courted with notes delivered by Frank, and secret meetings. Finally, when their young hearts had reached their peaks of tolerance, they slipped away and were married in a double ceremony with another of Leness' friends, Burt Hamilton, who married Rosie Keith.

Afraid to return home, Len and Martha pitched a tent on the banks of the Buffalo River and lived in romantic seclusion until Tommy and Susie found them. They were happily surprised when Tommy and Susie insisted they both come home with them. A lifelong friendship began that day between Len and his father-in-law.

In a few years, Len built a good house a short distance up the mountain from Tommy and Susie, for his growing family. Behind the house was an excellent spring of water and from the long front porch, Martha could see range after range of her beloved Ozark Mountains.

All too soon, Martha's mother began to suffer from an undetermined illness. Tommy had many doctors come to her bedside but all to no avail. Doc Southerlin stayed by her bed until the end. Only fifty-three, she breathed her last. Tommy's grief was overwhelming and he was never the same until the day of his death. He simply could not accept his loss and followed her a few short years later to his final reward.

The hills rang with sorrow for the loss of two fine people. They would miss Tommy Baker, so gallant and businesslike in his starched and ironed white shirts and mounted on the best saddle horse around. They would miss little Susie, who loved everybody and wanted to be assured only of her family and friends' comfort when they were near her.

Into Martha had been instilled this complete unselfishness.

Martha was crushed by the loss of her parents, but soon was able to accept it as inevitable and busied herself with caring for her family, which was growing up and leaving them.

Martha and Leness had five children, one of whom died in infancy. Mamie, Mildred, Tommy and Bonnie House were all reared with the same kind of love Martha had known. Len was a good provider. He ran many head of hogs, cattle, milk goats and chickens.

As fate would have it, after living in the same place for forty-five years, Martha was to be uprooted from her recluse on the mountain. She was faced with the terrible realization that she would have to leave. Len had lost both legs as a result of diabetes and spent many weeks in the VA Hospital in Little Rock.

Martha was crushed by the turn of events, but knew she could not whine nor complain. She had to be brave for Len and her children. Being from pioneer stock, she managed to smile, even though her heart was crumbling.

Later, still more suffering was in store for Martha. She fell and broke her hip. But neither could this keep her down for long. She was soon able to walk with the aid of a cane.

She keeps up her courage through her strong faith in God. She told me sadly that nothing seems the same since leaving Ponca (just as Frank Villines has said) and that even the whipporwill's song sounds different when they give their plaintive cry.

Martha is one of the most courageous women I have ever known. She displays a keen intelligence and a wholesome love for everyone. I feel warm and happy when I am around her.

As her mother before her, she gets her greatest pleasure out of doing for other people, especially preparing a festive meal for anyone who comes to call. Just like the Martha in the Bible who was so intent and anxious to serve our Lord.

One day, she and I were talking about death and meeting our maker. She said quickly, "Why, I wouldn't be afraid if someone said Jesus was out in that yard." I laughed and hugged her. "I know," I said, "You'd want someone to go get him and bring him in so you could feed him."

I love you, Martha Baker House.

On September 6, 1977, Leness House passed away. He and Martha had celebrated their 60th wedding anniversary in July. It will be most difficult for her to adjust since her life was wrapped totally and unselfishly around that man whom she loved with all her strength. Since he had been an invalid for many years, she had the responsibility of caring for him and it will be a task for her to shuffle her thoughts and actions without him. As she so beautifully put it on the day Len was buried, "God will just have to help me." And He will, I know.

BOXLEY JOE

"There are in the world two powers — the sword and the spirit. The spirit has always vanquished the sword."

— Napoleon

Joseph Villines, also known as "Boxley Joe" was an outstanding citizen of the Boxley Community. He was a shrewd businessman and had a good mercantile store at Boxley and extensive real estate holdings.

Joe was born April 19, 1849 in Boxley where he lived all but the last three years of his life. He was the son of Hosea (son of Hezekiah) and Lucinda Cecil Villines. He was postmaster at Boxley from 1891 to 1911.

In 1875 he married Bell McCracken and to them sixteen children were bom, eleven of whom survived him at his death in 1913. There were Lon,

Harve, Walter, Sid, Roy, Sneed, Claud, Mrs. Carroll Stafford, Misses Laura and Jessie Villines and Mrs. Newt Blackwood.

As a result of a short fued like situation in 1910, a Mr. Walker was killed at the Boxley store and Joe Villines was involved. There was such controversy and ill feelings, even after Joe's acquittal, that he found it necessary to move his family to Green Forest, Arkansas and start a new life.

In Green Forest, he became active in civic affairs and once more delved into the mercantile and real estate business.

While on a business trip to Marshall, Arkansas, he suffered a heart attack and died. In the lengthy obituary, the editor of the Green Forest Tribune gave an account in reference to the killing; it appears in part as follows:

. . During the ordeal through which he passed in his trouble over the Walker killing in 1910, he often talked freely to us and we do not now recall that he ever gave utterance of an unkind thought against those who fought so hard to deprive <u>him</u> of his freedom. He spoke often in the strongest terms of appreciation of the friends who came so spontaneously and in such numbers to his aid, saying that this expression was a rift that almost dispelled the clouds that hung so heavily over him and his family. The ravages of worry told on him, however, each month of this crisis adding a year to his age and there is little doubt that this unfortunate circumstance had much to do in hastening him to his grave. This is an occasion where the writer's ability of expression fails him and his vision is dimmed with tears of sorrow for the loss of so good a friend and citizen . .

. . In the death of Joseph Villines, the Tribune has lost one of its most valuable friends, for he was enterprising, every inch of him. In this respect his life stood out boldly in contrast with that of many of the old timers of this country, all of whom were schooled in a species of economy that in after years has generally developed into closefistedness.

Our estimate of Mr. Villines, after a more or less intimate acquaintance with him for some years, is that he was truly one of God's noblemen, possessing more of the attributes of true manhood than ordinarily falls to the fortune of one individual . .

(Green Forest Tribune — October 31, 1913)

THE GENTLE YANKEE

His life was gentle, and elements So mix'd in him that nature might stand up and say to all the world, "This was a man!"
— Shakespeare's Julius Caesar

Frank Villines fondly remembers a true gentleman and friend, Jess Shroll, the nice looking yankee who found a good life and made a multitude of friends in Newton County.

Jess came to the hills from Ohio, where he left a childhood sweetheart and an anxious family. His mother wanted him to return to Ohio, and being of some financial means, offered to buy him one of the finest farms in the state.

But Jess didn't want the finest farm in Ohio. He chose instead the quiet hills of Newton County, Arkansas where the sincere and friendly hill people warmed his very heart.

He looked at the huge white oak timber standing tall and silent all about him, and made plans to one day own a saw<u>mill</u>.

He first took his savings and went partners with Fate Edgmon in a general store at Boxley, Arkansas. Here, he learned to know and respect the ways of hillfolk.

Jess had a college education and used his gained knowledge to help his friends in their business encounters, such as figuring out property lines and other ventures. For some of his beloved friends, some of whom had not had the advantages Jess had, he wrote letters, speeches and sermons and helped solve any problem he could. He seemed to take everyone under his wing and found complete contentment in so doing.

He was a quiet man who never wasted words. He enjoyed taking a few drinks with his friends. Only then would he open up and talk of his childhood sweetheart; how they drove the cows to pasture each morning on their way to school; how pretty she was and that he picked a wild rose for her hair. He then told of a dream that he had of he and she dying and driving cows to pasture in heaven. Just days after telling the dream, a letter came from his mother telling him that his sweetheart had died suddenly. He recollected that it was the same night he dreamt of their deaths. He told the story many times afterwards to his friends.

Soon, Jess had his sawmills where he cut wagon tongues, lumber and cuts for the latest thing in veneer called "flitch- wood." After these beautifully

70

grained cuts left Jess' mill, they were re-sawed very thin and glued to furniture, giving it a solid oak appearance.

He bought much land around Ponca and Boxley and planted apple trees on some of it. Those trees are to this day still bearing fruit. The sturdy rock springhouse stands as it did the day he built it on the road going toward Lost Valley.

Civic minded Jess wanted good things for his community and was one of the road commissioners instrumental in getting the road built to Ponca and vicinity. He and Laddie Boone went to Ohio and brought back two of the first automobiles, a Reo and a Ford. Jess kept the Ford and sold the Reo to Tommy Baker for six hundred dollars. The Reo was comparable to one of the higher priced big cars of today. About that same time, Tom Chaffin had another Ford in Ponca.

Jess courted and married Mamie Blank, a polished young lady who could match wits with Jess. He loved her dearly, but as fate would have it, she died in the Flu Epidemic of 1918, leaving Jess and their young son, Robert. Mamie's sister and her husband, Lizzie and Ed Minnicus opened their arms to Robert and raised him as their own.

Later, Jess married Josie Isler, a young widow with whom he had ten happy years before his death.

When Jess Shroll came to the hills of Northwest Arkansas, he, like many young men, was searching for something. He found his dream in the Ozarks where he also found respect and more friends than most men have who live many years longer than Jess did.

He loved and served his community every day he lived and the hills were saddened when he died suddenly from a heart condition on November 1, 1938. Josie, understanding woman she was, had her husband buried by his first wife, Mamie in the Beechwood Cemetery.

Jess Shroll rests in the hills he loved. Ask any old timer about him and he'll lean back and take on a pleasant, faraway look as he remembers. Jess held a special place in the hearts and minds of all who knew him — the gentle Yankee.

LITTLE GOAT LADY OF CENTER POINT

"The attributes of a great lady may still be found in the rule of the four S's Sincerity, Simplicity, Sympathy, Serenity."

— Emily Post

Newton County has many pioneer women. Women who can tolerate more pain, deprivation and disillusionment than can be imagined by most of us. Mountain women are made to last. It's as if they are competing with the rock hardness of the surrounding hills. They, like the hills, are indestructible.

One such woman is Eva Barnes Henderson. Standing stretched on tiptoe, she might reach the five foot mark. But don't be fooled by her size.

Eva Barnes was born in Newton County just a few miles from where she has lived for over three quarters of a century at Center Point (this location is discussed elsewhere in the book). She was one of nine children born to Susie Buchanan Barnes, grandniece of James Buchanan, 15th president of the United States and John "Jonk" Barnes.

When Eva was fourteen months old, her father died. Susie Barnes grieved for as long as she felt possible and then went about the business of rearing her children. There was no social security, welfare program nor food stamps. She knew of no other way to keep food in their mouths except to work and teach them to do likewise.

Eva married Frank Henderson when she was sixteen years old and they built a little house near the one in which Eva presently lives. To this union, two children were bom, one of whom died from a fever while an infant. The other, Arbie Henderson, married Ray Villines, half-brother to Frank Villines. Their descendants are listed at the end of this biography.

Eva stayed at her husband's side doing a man's share of the hard work. Together, they made a good living from the land.

Eva loved goats and was able to get her a start of milkers. They multiplied rapidly and soon she lost count of just how many she did have. They roamed the lush benches and bluffs where they found plenty of greens to eat. Along about milking time, Eva went in search of them. She climbed over boulders and up rocky bluffs almost as agile as her goats in search of a missing doe about to kid. She drove them home and milked them all even if they gave no more than a cupful. At one time, she was milking thirty-five goats twice a day and seven cows. This was while her husband was still living. Together they separated the cream and stored it in the cool rocky cellar until the day they took it to the creamery which was then in Harrison, Arkansas.

Eva no longer has goats, but runs a nice herd of whitefaced cows and a number of hogs and some two hundred chickens. It takes a large part of her day to feed and care for her stock. In the dry part of the year, she carries water from the Buffalo rivgr to the cows. A trail has been worn smooth from the river to the fence where she pours the filled buckets over into a watering trough to her thirsty, spoiled cows.

Recently, one of her cows was ailing and needed a shot. She didn't think it wise to wait until someone came down to mountain to help her. The cow naturally objected and knocked the needle and medicine "winding." Eva patiently got more medicine, cleaned up the needle and hobbled the cow saying quietly: "We gonna give you that shot if it takes all day." She then tied the cow and gave her the shot. This particular cow no longer has a great affection for Eva and looks warily at her each time she comes near to see if she's sporting a long needle.

When a cow needs drenching, Eva hobbles and ties her and away she goes. This is probably very humorous to see this small woman manhandling a giant cow.

She also assists in the birth of their calves if such help is needed and "sits up" with them if they are having a bad time of it.

She raises some of the finest hogs around and soaks the hybrid corn, since it is very hard, for them to eat. Her kindness to animals is heartwarming.

I looked about as I talked with this unusual lady. She has flowers indoors and says she can't put them outside as the animals will destroy them. There is no electricity and several kerosene filled lamps with trimmed wicks were here and there. I noticed an Open Bible on a little table beside her bed.

I asked if she was ever lonesome, to which she replied, "Lan' sakes, no, I don't have time for that." I let those very wise words soak in as I looked at the muscled legs and straight shoulders of this woman in her eighties. Her robust health, in all likelihood, is due to the fact that she stays busy and "doesn't have time" to be lonely.

Eva's place, just a few hundred yards from Sneed Creek of the Buffalo River, is reached by turning off the road near Compton leading down the mountain to Center Point, where many years ago, a well-known- school by that name, with many students was in session.

One must blink their eyes to believe the rugged beauty of the hills in this area and it is not very far at all from Eva's house where it is believed the very first Villines hunters camped on the big flat rock and fought the panther before returning to their native lands and bringing back their families.

Eva's place is quiet and peaceful for the most part. However, since the park has taken over, there is a considerable amount of traffic in the tourist season, but Eva doesn't mind and says, "long as they don't bother me" and "mind their own business."

On down from Eva's place one can reach Hemmed in Hollow by being in the mood for climbing or wading the creek several time. A chapter on this area is included.

Several years ago, Eva had a big black and white dog which had a lot of shepherd breeding. He was her first love and protection. She told of a time when he saved her life. A wild boar with tusks barred charged her and knocked her sailing through the air. He started for a repeat performance while Eva was still down but Donnie tore into him sending him on his way back into the hills. She still talks of him frequently and it grieved her to no end when he died. She has another dog now who she named "Bobbie" but she declares he is not as smart as Donnie was "but he's learning."

Eva's daughter and grandchildren were concerned about her living alone with no telephone or car and talked her into buying a little place near them at Compton. But she couldn't leave. How does one leave a place where they have lived all their life, a place that is much a part of them as the rocks in the creek bed. She told them she would surely die if she left her home and all her animals.

This is the Little Goat Lady of Center Point

— a real lady.

This is Eva Barnes Henderson, her daughter Arbie and

Arbie's husband Ray (Frank's brother) and their children.

Eva's daughter, Arbie Henderson Villines, married Ray
Villines and to that union nine children were born:
Howard Villines, bom January 14, 1930 — married Betty Sims Freeda
Villines, born 12-29-31, married to Garland Martin
Erma Villines, bom 11-22-33, married to Ebert Gibbins
Ruby Villines, born 9-25-35, married to Leon Gray
Cleo Villines, born 1-20-38, married to Riner Gibbins
Perry Villines, born 5-1-40, married to Sylvinia Willis
Wilma Villines, bom 4-11-43, married to Louis Sims
Marie Villines bom 11-9-45, married to Gerry Bryant
Jane Villines, bom 6-26-48, married to Hillard Kilgore

Ray Villines digging potatoes with the mule that he bought
in 1934.

Ray Villines digs potatoes with the family mule, now 44 years old. (or older) He told me that he bought the mule in 1934 from Jim Farmer and farmed him all the time they lived on the "creek." The last fifteen years, they have just made gardens with him.

V

... AND THERE WERE HAPPENINGS

. . Under the spreading chestnut tree The village smithy stands;
The smith, a mighty man is he,
With large and sinewy hands;
And the muscles of his brawny arms Are strong as iron bands.
He earns whate'er he can,
And looks the whole world in the face.
For he owes not any man.
Toiling, — rejoicing, — sorrowing,
Onward through life he goes;
But each morning sees some task begin,
Each evening sees it close;
Something attempted, something done,
Has earned a night's repose.

The Village Blacksmith
Henry Wordsworth Longfellow

Blacksmithing in Newton County

The fine art of blacksmithing, with the exception of horse shoe making, is dying out. Only a few old timers can perform this once highly essential trade. They will soon be gone, and unless their knowledge and art is passed on to another generation, the art will belong to the glorious past.

It's interesting to note that in 1850 according to the U.S. Census report for Newton County, there were eight blacksmiths in the county as follows:

HEAD OF HOUSEHOLD BORN OCCUPATION
T. C. Jones Tennessee Blacksmith
Nathan Flud NorthCarolina Blacksmith
Carter Wells Tennessee Blacksmith

Edward Williams Tennessee Blacksmith
Samuel Kelly North Carolina Blacksmith
Jesse E. Casey Georgia Blacksmith
William H. Parker Kentucky Blacksmith
Nathanial Bunch Virginia Blacksmith

In *1860,* the population had increased and so had the number of blacksmiths. Now, there were eighteen "smiths" in the county as follows:

HEAD OF HOUSEHOLD BORN OCCUPATION
James Vanderpool Indiana Blacksmith
William Brisco Alabama Blacksmith
Elisha GreenTennessee Blacksmith
John Sumpter North Carolina Blacksmith
John Adare (Adair) Tennessee Blacksmith
Shed Dunn Illinois Blacksmith
William Evans Alabama Blacksmith
Thomas Nelson North Carolina Blacksmith
Andrew J. Clements Missouri Blacksmith
John Allred Tennessee Blacksmith
W. P. Allred Tennessee Blacksmith
John Thomas Kentucky Blacksmith
James Lee Virginia Blacksmith
Thomas Shatswel Massachusetts Blacksmith
S. 0. Standridge Arkansas Blacksmith
W. J. Warren Tennessee Blacksmith
Isaac Adams North Carolina Blacksmith
Absolum Manna Kentucky Blacksmith

These blacksmiths were spread out over the county with one or two in every community. These men made a living at blacksmithing, but many of the farmers in Newton County learned the art for convenience sake. When they broke a plow they did not have time to travel perhaps ten or fifteen miles to the nearest blacksmith, but it was necessary to learn at least the rudiments of the trade to get by. His "shop" was probably an area near the bam over a large natural rock floor. Here, he had a small forge, an anvil, several hammers and pairs of tongs, and odds and bits of iron and a large basket of charcoal. He could make horse shoes, repair and make some of his farm tools, and fashion a fair set of dog irons for the fireplace.

The local blacksmith shop was often the meeting place of the tradesmen. The farmer watched and asked question, which the overworked blacksmith was always glad to answer. And this is how he learned enough about the art to "get by." Once learned, he probably passed his knowledge onto his sons, some of whom became artisans in the field of blacksmithing.

Frank Villines knows blacksmithing and learned also by observation. He still fires up the little forge in his garage and makes very artistic fish gigs and garden tools. He also repairs various tools occasionally.

Gas and electric welding, tool and die-making shops, rolling and forging mills of the steel industry have all but eliminated the need to learn blacksmithing and this is unfortunate since it is truly a work of art.

Other Arts of the Past

Do you know what a Cooper is? A cooper was a skilled worker who had the knowledge of making and repairing barrels and casks.

Now, this work is done in factories, and one doesn't see wooden barrels as they once did. Wooden barrels and kegs now, for the most part, are used only in the distilling of whiskey.

Tbere is a stave mill in neighboring Boone County where staves for whiskey barrels are made. Stave mills were quite common in the early days of Newton County since barrels and kegs were used almost exclusively for storage of all kinds.

But the cooper made the barrels by hand and they were guaranteed not to leak for as long as they held together. At the turn of the century, Frank Villines said there were a dozen or more coopers in Newton County, but today, it is an unheard of art.

In the 1850 Census Report, there were two coopers: John Bradford from South Carolina and George Workman from Tennessee. In the 1860 Census Report, there are two which appears to be a man and his son, Richard Coleman, bom in North Carolina and John Coleman, bom in Indiana.

Those two Census Records reveal some interesting trades and arts. There were understandably many wagon makers; also, a number of chair makers were listed.

Recently, I noticed some beautiful rocking and straight chairs in a local hardware store in Newton County. The proprietor said the walnut beauties were made by a man "up on the mountain." I asked if he had passed the art down to his sons and he said, no, his sons were not interested in it. The chairs were inexpensive and so tasteful any home would be proud to have one.

He told me there were only three chair makers left in the county and all were older men who had no one to whom they could leave the knowledge of their craft. So, another beautiful art will die when these gentlemen make their last sturdy chair from the raw materials found in their midsts.

In that long ago record, other interesting arts listed were sawyers, teamsters, mechanics (for what, I wonder), millers, wheel wrights, shoemakers, boot makers and one hatter. There were only three carpenters listed, so most people probably did their own building.

Fortunately, there are annual arts and crafts festivals held in literally every county of the Ozarks, where one can observe people busy making items with their hands such as wagons, guns, baskets, barrels, chairs and many, many more. These festivals are highly publicized and perhaps in this way, many of the beautiful arts so fast succumbing before the onslaught of the mighty machine and ghastly automation, will be kept alive for a time anyway.

And who knows, there may be a future time (and perhaps not so distant future) when many of us will have a real need to know how to perform these ancient crafts in order to survive.

Mining in Newton County

Deep in unfathomable mines of never failing skill God treasures up his bright designs and works his soverign will

— William Cowper

Crude, gouged out openings in the hillsides around Ponca indicate very early lead mining in Newton County; probably for the purpose of making bullets. Some military records report that during the Civil War large smelters were set up in the valley for melting lead that had been taken from outcroppings on Steel Creek, Panther Creek and others. After the war there was much talk about a lost lead mine up Steel Creek which was used during the Civil War, but it was not found during the mining boom in the area in the 1890's. There are men living today who declare that they heard their ancestors speak of that rich outcropping of lead up Steel Creek and that they know it was not just a legend. Many have looked for it before and since but none have found it.

Martha House tells of two lead molds which her father, Tommy Baker brought home from the old Civil War smelters when they were tom down. They were used for years as watering troughs for the chickens and in fact, her son, Tommy, now has one in his possession. The molds are V- shaped, solid iron and very heavy, and about twenty-four inches long and six inches deep. The molten lead was poured from the smelters into these molds to solidify. The block of pure lead weighed exactly eighty pounds and was called a "pig of lead." The mold itself was also called a pig. Once the lead had been initially melted, it could be melted again at a lower temperature and cast into bullets and minie balls.

Many old mountain men, not wanting to divulge the secret location of their lead supply for bullets long ago, told no one of their whereabouts. Eventually many rich veins were lost forever as was the Steel Creek outcropping.

Later, speculators, aware of lead and zinc deposits in Newton County came in and bought up or leased much of the land.

One such speculator was Martha Baker House's grandfather Baker. Later, when tests revealed a high percentage of lead and zinc, mining companies came into the area and leased up every available foot of land from the Bakers and others in and around Ponca. The fact is, Ponca was named after Ponca City Mining Company out of Ponca City, Oklahoma when it came in the area and opened the mines.

The quiet little community of a handful of people became a buzzing boom town with a population of many hundreds. An endless train of wagons loaded with mining equipment and supplies poured into Newton County. Mining camps sprang up overnight and tents and shacks dotted every hillside. A large hotel eventually opened and room and board was had for fifty cents a day.

The mines flourished for quite a few years and the production and value of metallic zinc and lead reached its highest in 1916 and 1917. During this period, the average price of sphalerite concentrate (zinc sulphide 67.1 percent zinc, usually brownish-yellow to yellow-green and having a resinous luster) rose from $26.12 to $68.21 per short ton and Galena (lead) from $46.31 to $110.41 per short ton.

Times were good for Newton County and Frank Villines. Another means of extra money came into play and Frank took advantage of it.

He joined Leness House, donned his carbide lamp and pick and went to work for ten hours a day in the mines for $1.50. Big money for the young, burly fellows who didn't tire easily. After working a full ten bours, they still had the energy to go down to the creek and catch a mess of fish which they took to their boarding house and had the lady of the house cook for supper. All along the way from the creek, fellow workers hollered at the pair trying to get them to sell their fish to them, but Len and Frank already had their taste buds fired up, so they just laughed, shook their heads and yelled back for them to go catch their own.

Frank and Len worked side by side in the mines for two years and had many harrowing and humorous experiences to relate.

Once Frank had been lowered into a shaft to set off a charge of dynamite and as soon as the fuse was lighted, he yelled to be pulled up. His hoisters were a mite slow and the explosion impact ripped off the heel of Frank's shoe as he reached the top.

Another time, a huge boulder got away and began tumbling in Len's direction. Frank yelled at him; he turned around and all but melted into a hollowed out spot in the mine wall. Only sheer imagination was left for room between rock and man. Len had to skin out of his pants before he could slither from behind his rock prison. After he was free and checked for injuries, everyone roared with laughter. When they were telling this story to me, they laughed until tears ran down their faces.

One night, Frank and Len went bird thrashing. They had their carbide lamps fastened to their caps and were armed with good stout sticks. Suddenly, a big red bird headed for a cedar thicket. Len was in the lead thrashing away and suddenly, Frank heard him yell for help. Frank followed his voice in the dark and his frantic cries seemed to be coming from down under. He shone his light into Len's big frightened eyes. He had fallen into an old mine shaft quite a few feet deep and was up to his waist in water. He kept saying, "Where the hell am I?" Frank asked if he was hurt and he said he reckoned not. Then, Frank sat back on his heels and laughed until tears rolled. This didn't set too well with Len and he told him so in a few choice words. Frank enjoyed his mirth and then sat about cutting a long sapling pole to help his friend out of his watery trap. Before their night of bird thrashing was over, Frank almost fell into the same hole. The only one sorry he didn't was Len.

One day after two years of working in the mines, Frank and Len talked as they worked:

"Len, ain't you 'bout tired of working under the ground like a mole?"

Frank pounded the spike as he spoke and a smile played at the corners of his mouth.

"Yeah, I 'bout had a gracious plenty of it. Why?"

"What say we drag up. The war's gonna get us before long anyhow. Let's ring that bell for the last time and have 'em haul us out of here."

"Suits me."

Both men were grinning by now and Frank reached for the bell.

Once outside they drew their pay and the two young mountain men went their merry ways deep into the hills of Newton County in search of further adventures.

Leness House and Burt Hamilton worked in the mines a good while before Frank joined them. They were subleasing a job to remove lead from a shaft that had been sunk by some ruthless fellows. The scoundrels had found a large amount of lead, but simply left it there when Tommy Baker refused to renew their lease. Tommy let Len and Burt have the sub-lease. They found the ore left by the crooks as well as twenty-eight more tons which Len discovered when he poked his curious head through a small opening in the shaft. Burt yelled like a stuck pig when Len showed it to him. The two happy young men had struck a small fortune since ore that rich was bringing $120.00 per ton.

The mining boom soon fizzled out but it had its day. There were many mines in the area, but one in particular has an interesting history, the Panther Creek Mine:

Panther Creek got its name when one of Newton County's first settlers, Samuel Hudson, killed a panther well up above where the Panther Creek mines were later located. It seems the story of Hudson and the panther has been handed down through the years and those who tell it declare it not to be a legend but the gospel truth. It goes thus:

Hudson and one of his sons were out robbing bee trees and when they had finished their chore, they started home with their filled pails of honey. The panther smelled the honey and came near. Hudson had the ax he had used to cut the bee tree and threw it at the panther but missed his target. The panther sprang and man and beast were in a life and death struggle. Hudson yelled to his son to hand him the butcher knife they had used to cut the comb from the honey tree and the lad passed it to him. Hudson slashed the panther again and again finally killing him. They took the panther home and skinned him to keep the hide but there were so many cuts in the hide that it was not a pretty sight. The panther measured nine feet from nose to tip of tail.

Afterwards, the creek along the way Hudson and his son had travelled was named Panther Creek and is so known to this day.

It seems that lead ore on Panther Creek was discovered quite by accident. A young man, namely Jasper Rush, who lived near the rough terrain, was digging for ginseng roots on a rock ledge and his eyes caught a glistening substance where he had broken through with his hoe. Soon every miner and prospector around knew of the find and the terrain up and down Panther Creek area was a miner's paradise.

From the records, it seems that Jackson Kilgore along with his brother, Issac Kilgore, Jesse Kir, Sid Allen and some other early miners put the Panther Creek mine on the map when they quarried a big block of "jack" lead ore. So outstanding was the ore that they decided to send it all the way to the World's Fair in St. Louis, Missouri. It won first honors in its class and was on display there for years to come.

For sixty years or so Panther Creek Mines were worked and many thousands of dollars of ore were sold. The biggest drawback was the transportation or lack of it in getting the ore to market.

The Panther Creek mine area and valley are breath- takingly beautiful and can be reached from the famous Diamond Cave by following the old C.C.C. Road up Henson Creek about two miles until you reach the foot of the mountain. Here, one turns right on the old wagon road (if it is still visible) up

Panther Creek Valley. Each step up this beautiful valley is utterly fascinating with its pine and hardwood timber on steep hillsides and bluffs down to the bottom of the creek bed. If one chooses to explore the area, it would be wise to have someone escort them through this still primitive area as it would be quite simple to get hopelessly lost if the creek bed were left. Also check with landowners for permission to trek their lands.

Changing Shifts at the Mines
Elmer Southerland, Fagan Walker and Jim Blackston.

The following is a list of production and mines in Newton County of lead and zinc concentrates as it appears in "Mineral Resources of Arkansas dated 1927."

SHIPMENT OF LEAD CONCENTRATES
Ike Kilgore 412,000lbs.
Minicus and Villines 140,000lbs.
Hamilton and Young 218,000lbs.
L. E. Lake 150,000lbs.
Bald Hill Mining Company 50,000lbs.
North Slope Mining Company 50,000lbs.
L. L. Brown 10,000lbs.
A. J. Wassel 4,000lbs.
Miscellaneous 130,000lbs.
TOTAL 1,164,000lbs.

SHIPMENTS OF ZINC CONCENTRATES
North Slope Mining Company 1,745,000lbs.
Bald Hill Mining Company 410,000lbs.
Hamilton and White 228,000lbs.
Eleventh Hour Mining Company 460,000lbs.
Van Sickles 214,000lbs.
Victor Primrose 890,000lbs.
Cook & McCoy 490,000lbs.
E.R. Springer 160,000lbs.
W. N. North 100,000lbs.
L. E. Lake 60,000lbs.
M. G. Moss 228,000lbs.
W. E. Luke 120,000lbs.
Hamilton & Young 60,000lbs.
Miscellaneous 1,510,000lbs.
TOTAL 5,417,000lbs.

Some of the Cedar Timber Crew –
Frank Villines, Will Culbertson,
Calvin Eoff, Jasper Eoff, Mack Eoff 1907

The Cedar Harvest

Wine that maketh glad the hearts of man; and oil to make him a cheerful countenance, and bread to strengthen man's heart.
The trees of the Lord also are full of sap; even the cedars of Libanus which He hath planted.

— The Book of Common Prayer

The first "big money" remembered by ole timers in Newton County came from the cedar harvests and cedar floats.

Around the turn of the century red cedar timber flourished along the banks of the Buffalo River and for many thousands of acres beyond. This was virgin timber, rich and towering on the hill slopes.

In Florida, cedar timber harvesting had its beginning around 1880. As the cedar was thinned out, cedar buyers moved west. Northwest Arkansas was chosen last because of transportation facilities. The harvest in Newton County began about 1903 with the Eagle Pencil Company piloting the operation. Remember the penny cedar pencils?

Frank Villines applied for a job cutting timber, and it was a stroke of luck to find work in his own front yard. He gazed long at all the red cedar timber and thought how he had been watching it all his life and not once had thought of its monetary value. Now, he was about to get paid a dollar a day and eats for cutting and snaking out logs.

In a cedar harvest, the mule is the most indispensable item around. There were lots of good mules in those cedar cutting years. Cedar logs were tied to mules and they started downhill, sidestepping when the log crowded them. They instinctively knew the danger. Most of the mules were as graceful as any ballet dancer, but not by choice. It was that or be maimed by a rushing log and destroyed. The mule skinner walked alongside the mule and did his best to keep the log from hanging on underbrush or exposed tree roots.

Cedar cutting was a giant enterprise and naturally, everyone wanted a piece of the action. Running such a business required planning and ingenuity on the parts of many minds.

The foreman was responsible for seeing that things ran as smoothly as possible. He saw that the saws and axes were kept razor sharp, that plenty of good mules were on hand, that enough men were hired to make up a good crew and a multitude of other tasks.

Frank liked his work cutting timber as it kept him in the great outdoors. He drank in the hum of activity, the yelling of the men at their mules and the ring of many axes and sing-song of crosscut saws. He relished the invigorating, rich smell of fresh cut virgin cedar logs.

He also enjoyed the fellowship of his co-workers. They joshed one another until it was a crying shame and hard laughter wrung tears from the ej'es of those sturdy mountain men who took part in the jokes.

Some of the men who worked with Frank during the 1904 and 1905 were: Jess and Tim Thompson, Tom and Will Culbertson, Jack Brooks, Jal Reed, Tom Harding, Carl Beasley, Eh Simmons, Jess Crawford, Bill Bailey, Elie May, Lon Trigger, Henry Barnett and A. L. May. The foremen then were John and 0. K. Kennedy. There were many others who came and went in a hurry for a variety of reasons.

Frank was very fond of Mrs. Susie Barnes (mother of Eva Barnes Henderson) who cooked for the timber harvesting crew four years off and on. She was like a mother to Frank and the others.

Mrs. Barnes rose at three in the morning to begin breakfast. What a chore it must have been to cook enough biscuits, sausage, side meat, eggs and coffee for that crew of hungry mountain boys. They all helped by keeping plenty of dry cedar limbs and chips and water handy.

As soon as breakfast was eaten and dishes done, it was time to begin lunch, which consisted of huge pots of beans, potatoes, pork meat and the like. The company bought any fresh vegetables in season from the local people, as well as eggs and meat. The Eagle Pencil Company believed in feeding its men, but it also believed in a good day's work in return.

When the crew was cutting some distance from the cook tent, the hot food was transported by wagon and team to the men high in the cedar brakes.

It was a long, hard day for Mrs. Barnes and some of her older children, but she always managed to bake a big batch of pies two or three times a week. She was never too tired to sew on a button or patch a pair of overalls for one of "her boys." It's no wonder they all loved her, and that her boss considered her invaluable to the cutting operation.

A Mr. McQuitty and his wife operated a commissary in a large tent. Here one could buy axes, saw handles, files, overalls, boots, tobacco and a few sweet treats. Mr. McQuitty followed the timber crew all the way down the river. When they broke camp, he followed.

The cedar logs were placed and stacked on the river bank in "yards" to wait for the right time to start floating. The logs were cut in lengths of twelve feet. The yards were always in the most convenient locations to get them in the river when the water "got right."

Logs were never put in when the river was rising as the current kept pushing them to the bank where they landed up in trees and boulders on the bank. On the other hand, when the river was going down, the pull was toward the middle and this gave the floaters command of the logs. Floats were usually started in the spring or fall, and the right time was governed by the river's stage.

Frank always felt excitement when the foreman put his hands to the sides of his mouth and bellowed, "Let's put 'em in the water." The sound of stakes snapping and logs rumbling, sometimes over a fairly steep bluff, and the splash and spray of water many feet high, was indeed a phenomena for a young man such as Frank Villines. Often, however, the yards were right on the river and did not house neat stacks, but just a huge debris of logs waiting for the heave and strength of men to put them into the water. This was a real show of strength, and where possible, spectators from the nearby villages and houses came to watch this display of brawn.

The men jumped in the water as if it were dry land to straighten logs and untangle some. They yelled, laughed, cursed and sang. It was a good life!

Late fall and early spring in Newton County can bring some "mean" weather without much warning. Flash floods can send ole Buffalo into a frenzy to get out of her banks within an hour. Many times ice formed on Frank's wet clothes after a hard fall freeze. He would be numb for hours from the biting wind. But someone always had a bottle to warm the blood and stave off a bad cold in those bad times.

When the weather was extremely cold, it was difficult to keep a crew. No one could blame the men, though, as it was much nicer to be home with the family before a crackling fire than in a tent that leaked and was never really warm.

However, Frank's youth, vigor and the way Ab Villines raised him caused the word "quit" to never enter his mind. He was there to harvest cedar timber and harvest it he would.

Before Frank's cedar work played out, he'd just about tackled every job offered even down to cooking on the floats.

He had never cooked much and his only experience had been in casually watching Mrs. Barnes back in the cutting camps as she skillfully rolled out uniform biscuits and placed them in the oven to bake. The only thing he hadn't noticed was exactly what she put in the biscuits besides flour. He knew some rising agent was used and salt, of course. These he added very generously to his flour and stirred it all up. He spooned several large biscuits unceremoniously into an iron spider. He put on a lid and began peeling the potatoes. Soon, he smelled bread baking and looking toward his skillet, he saw a sight to behold. The lid had risen up with the biscuits several inches and the whole ensemble resembled a ladies hat with roses on it. Needless to say, he wasn't asked to cook very often. But they all, including Frank, had a good belly laugh about Frank's biscuits.

Susie Buchanan Barnes, niece of President Buchanan, mother
of Eva Barnes Henderson, with husband whom she married
later in life, John Wilson.

On the floats, the men took turns washing dishes after the meals. This was a much disliked chore, but they took it like men and did their best. However, there was one tall, lanky, easy going fellow who refused absolutely and positively to wash dishes. He laughed at everything and never took anyone seriously, but "no siree, he would not wash dishes like no woman." Tbe man who took his turn at the dishes was pretty much miffed at him and wouldn't wash his plate.

Next morning at breakfast when vittles were being dipped into outstretched plates, the shirker laughed when he saw his dirty plate. He simply flipped his plate over and grinned, saying, "Put 'er right there, fellow."

Eating utensils like spoons and forks were always getting "borrowed" from eacb other and not finding their way home. Frank said most kept their spoons in their pockets but if it went missing, they just took their pocket knife and fashioned a spoon from wood.

The floats were hard and sometimes dangerous. Frank was rarely dry for the duration of a float and he and the others spent as much time in the water as out of it.

The biggest float Frank took part in was when 185,000 logs were floated to Gilbert down Buffalo. This float took twenty-two days. At its end, every muscle in Frank screamed for relief. It had been a grueling job for all the men to make the 185,000 logs behave in an unpredictable river. After the "big float" all the rest seemed like babies.

Vol Harrison worked, slept and ate with Frank for years in the cutting and floating of cedar logs. They were together at the end and hauled out the last two loads of cedar timber thrown into Buffalo.

Vol's father, Fletcher Harrison, a true pioneer, came to Newton County in 1848. The 1850 Newton County Census records show Fletcher to be two years old. Vol's grandfather, R. W. Harrison hailed from Tennessee and gave his occupation on the census as "lawyer."

After nine years in the cedar harvest, Frank felt he had contributed quite a bit of cedar for making penny pencils. And too, his life had also been enriched by tbis work, both financially and otherwise. He had learned a lot and was proud of it.

The 'Sang Hunters

To fill the hour, that is happiness.

Ralph Waldo Emerson

"Those Villines youngens can find more 'sang than anybody here abouts." **Those** words were repeated often in and around Low Gap, where Frank Villines was raised.

Frank's father spoke to the children: "It's too wet to hoe today, so you youngens just get your pouches and picks and go hunt 'sang. Look close, now, you hear?"

And look close they did. **An** older child who could recognize the valuable herb took along one or two smaller, inexperienced ones for the hunt. By the end of many crisp fall days, several pounds had been dug and put away to cure. The money realized from the ginseng would be used for extras and Christmas gifts.

What is Ginseng?

Ginseng is a peculiar herb and has been used for thousands of years for medicinal purposes. It takes the name from the Chinese words, "likeness of a man," because of the shape of the roots. They do, in fact, resemble the image of mankind.

Many records reveal that ginseng has been important in medicine in China and Tibet since as long ago as 196 A.D. It was described in an herbal of that date as "a tonic to the five viscera, quieting the spirits, establishing the soul, allaying fear, expelling evil effluvia, brightening the eyes, opening the heart, benefiting the understanding, and if taken for a long time, invigorating the body and prolonging life."

Ginseng is an herb that thrives in forested, sun-shaded areas of special soil. And that special soil is present in Newton County. It is of a plant family related to the ivy, but with dark, green leaves that are oval and pointed more like a maple leaf. It grows from seed whose long germination period does not produce a seedling for a year and a half. The plant brings up with it all the minerals from the soil and can be harvested only after six years of growth (or longer) so that its users will derive the most benefits. The old belief is that the older the root, the more potent it is.

The plant has five leaves, three large and two smaller ones. Its age can be determined by the number of prongs extending out from the stem. It is quite difficult to recognize because of its common look and resemblance to other weeds and plants.

After several years' growth the ginseng plant shows rich clusters of scarlet berries. The roots are then ready for gathering and the berries will provide seed. The roots range from four to eight inches long and wild ginseng is bringing nearly $80.00 per pound, all according to the shape, age, etc. When Frank Villines dug 'sang, it was bringing $2.00 per pound.

The Villines children knew none of the preceeding properties of ginseng; only that it was valuable and meant new shoes, boots, yard goods or a new pocket knife.

One wet, fall day, Frank's favorite little half-sister, Rossetta, trotted along carrying the pouch for him. She ran over thirty or forty yards away and snatched a brilliant cluster of berries and ran back to Frank to ask if it were 'sang. She couldn't remember where she got it and Frank scolded her for pulling the berries. She learned to bring Frank to the plant from then on.

Though Frank knew nothing then about preservation of this marketable root, as well as Golden Seal and others, common sense told him that if every sprig of the root were removed, the next few years would be barren ones for 'sang. They never dug roots from a young plant. This would be defeating their own purpose.

Frank no longer hunts 'sang but went with the author and her husband and taught us how to recognize it. Such a thrill to finally spot a healthy plant fifty yards away! But he does often use it medicinally. He still has 'sang and golden seal he gathered years ago and it still has it potentcy.

The fleshy roots of the wild ginseng in Newton County, as well as Golden Seal, have all but disappeared from the rich, damp hillsides. "Furriners" have come in and ruthlessly yanked up every root, some so small they wouldn't bring fifteen cents when cured.

It is raised commercially and the favorable climate and soil cause many thousands of dollars worth to be shipped from Newton County annually.

Now, since there is an acute awamess of preservation in the area, perhaps the 'sang like the cedar timber, will once again flourish in the county. Then, others can one day say to their offspring, "you youngens just go and hunt some 'sang today." I hope they will return with their pouches and every pocket brim full and overflowing.

Pettigrew Bound

To count the life of battle good,
And dear the land that gave you birth,
And dearer yet the brotherhood
That binds the brave of all the earth.

— Newbolt 1862-1938

Most Newton County husbandmen, including Frank's father, supported their families from the land. However, money was often needed for little extras. To obtain these, Ab Villines and others hauled freight and lumber in their wagons to the nearest railroad, at Petttigrew, Arkansas.

They began after the crop harvest when the cellar was bulging with apples, turnips, pumpkins and canned goods; and tbe smokehouse rafters sagging under the weight of cured hams and side meat.

Their freight was "turkey fat" (high grade zinc) and walnut lumber from the saw mill near Boxley, a little community in the western part of Newton County. The price for hauling was good - fifty cents per hundred feet for lumber. A good wagon could haul five hundred feet which meant $2.50 for a three day jaunt. The price for hauling ore brought about the same as it was figured by the hundredweight.

The three day round trip was often made under adverse weather conditions. The roads, filled with rocks and holes, were often icy and many times a heavy snow fell before their return.

The year was 1897. The season was the middle of winter. Ab Villines, his son-in-law, Henry Eoff and twelve-year-old Frank, bumped along in two wagons, loaded with turkey fat zinc.

The brakes were applied almost full-time to prevent the wagons from running over the mules as they descended the mountainous terrain of the Arkansas Ozarks.

Frank's big yellow cur, Watch, trotted alongside the wagons. Watch was a good wagon dog and kept the team peaceful by scaring away rabbits, snakes or anything which might spook the team. Often his presence meant fresh meat along the way as he pounced on a big cottontail and brought it to Frank. Frank was proud of Watch's reputation for having whipped three dogs at one time. It was simply the case of a boy loving a dog and a dog loving a boy.

The shadows of the pale December sun lengthened and it was time to seek shelter and rest the weary men and mules. They stopped at the old vacated Roper House on top of Winding Stair Mountain.

Inside they found a large pile of dry grass which probably had been dumped out of the bed tickings when the Ropers moved away. Over this pile of softness, they placed a wagon sheet for a bed. Frank carried an armload to the comer for Watch.

Next morning, Ab Villines got cold biscuits and streaked meat from the grub box in the wagon and warmed them on the fire and made scalding black coffee and they were ready to start out once more.

A winter wonderland greeted them as a heavy snow had fallen during the night. To Frank, it was beautiful, but it brought a furrow to Ab's brow as he knew driving would be even more hazardous and slow.

After a few hours Frank looked around for Watch and called him several times. His young heart sank as he remembered he hadn't let him out of the house after he fed him. Ab Villines looked at his son sadly. Frank knew without asking that they could not retrace those hard earned miles to release the dog. They'd have to get him on the return trip. Frank's day was mined as he thought of his big yellow dog whining to be set free to catch up with his wagons.

About the middle of the morning, they caught up with a regular "wagon train." The men and wagons were all from around Newton County. Frank counted twelve wagons loaded with first class walnut lumber headed for Pettigrew. He had never seen so many loaded wagons all at once.

Most of the men he had seen before and several of them were related to him. There was George Evans, Alf Keeton, Lon Villines, George Hale, Bob Walker and others. Not one man wore an overcoat in the near zero weather. One man had on overshoes, but the soles were "burned out" on them.

There was a fraternal brotherhood here. All these men were farmers and hill men. Men who knew only the hard life; men who never shirked a duty nor spent time complaining about things. They, like Frank's father, took life as it was handed them, the bad with the good.

Late that night, the men sat around a roaring fire and smoked, cursed, prayed, laughed a little and passed a bottle around. Most of the men had long beards and Frank saw little tags of ice in them glistening in the firelight.

They were camped on a little creek at the head of White River and were somewhat protected from the icy wind by the high bluffs. They had traveled a long distance over nearly impassable roads and trails for a pitiful sum of money. Yet, these gallant, uncomplaining men had guts and courage that wouldn't run out on them.

At Pettigrew, trains belched smoke and screeched their wheels causing the mules and horses to rare up and almost turn over the loaded wagons. Frank's eyes were wide with excitement as he beheld things he had never seen before: Ladies wearing their finery, getting on and off the trains; vendors selling their wares to passengers and spectators; and men carrying canes just for looks, wearing tall hats, heavy overcoats and shiny boots without holes. It was purely enough to make a boy like Frank dizzy with the thrill of it all.

Frank recalls on those trips gathering tin cans discarded by the town inhabitants. Cans were something Frank and his family didn't have and what wonderful containers they made for fishbait and for keeping treasures. He always divided them with the other children when he got home.

It was difficult to tell which was happier, boy or dog, when Watch was released from the old Roper house. He jumped straight up and licked Frank's face and then grabbed a big bite of snow to quench his two day thirst. It was a happy reunion on that return trip from Pettigrew.

On later trips, Frank, some years older, helped unhitch the teams when they came to iced over creeks and rivers. Here, the wagons were pushed across on the slick ice. The mules and horses were led down to places which weren't frozen where they waded across since they couldn't stand up on the ice.

In later years, Frank remembers when he and his good friend Frank Knight (son of Jack Knight) hired out to "Boxley Joe" (see index for biographical sketch) to haul walnut lumber from his mill at Boxley to Pettigrew. They were paid fifty cents a day for driving the wagons. Frank Knight was married to "Fishing Bill Villines" daughter, so this made him "kin" to Frank Villines.

Just before going down into the town of Pettigrew, there was a place called Red Star where they often camped. It was located on a bench of Red Star Mountain. Several abandoned houses and barns were used to get man and beast out of the weather. If all the shelters were taken, Frank and Frank Knight slept under the wagons. Frank declares that bench on Red Star Mountain was the coldest place in the world.

Frank doesn't dwell on the cold, the rain, the poorly clad men — what he does remember are the good times, the laughter, singing, the joshing of the men and the sheer thrill of just going somewhere; the excitement of seeing the long freight trains at Pettigrew and the "dressed up" folk there.

He remembers most of all the stalwart men from Newton County, working hard for a few extras for their families.

VI

AND THERE ARE PLACES...

"We do not count a man's years until he has nothing else to count."
— Ralph Waldo Emerson

Beechwood

There are many cemeteries in Newton County, some with unmarked rocks, the markings on many dimmed by time and others with bright, new stones of today.

Each has its share of Civil War graves. Most of these are unmarked but there are a few marked ones, much to the delight of a growing number of genealogists plodding through the cemeteries, squinting at the stones, pad in hand.

Each year a special day is set aside for decoration day. Former natives of the county and their descendants attend these gatherings from many parts of the country. The dates for these "Come Ins" are usually in the spring and fall, both beautiful seasons in the Ozarks.

Some take this day to collect for upkeep of the grounds. A good visit is had over a multitude of vittles spread on tables under the trees. But not before all have gone inside the nearby church for a good sermon and gospel singing.

The cemeteries are usually named for the churches nearby. At one time many churches served as schools during the week. One such was Beechwood. No one seems to know for certain, but it is assumed the church and cemetery were named for the many beech trees in the vicinity. Beechwood is located two miles from the Village of Ponca going toward Boxley just off Highway 43. Decoration Day at Beechwood is set each year on Mothers' Day.

Martha Baker House recalls some historical trivia about Beechwood. She remembers her father, Tommy Baker, gave a donation in about 1918 to "Ugly

Hez Villines" to buy lamps for the school/church. It seems he was going about collecting contributions for the building. ("Ugly Hez", as he was good-naturedly called, was the son of Jefferson Villines. "Ugly Hez" married Minnie Carlton. Then, of course, there was "Pretty Hez Villines", who was the son of James Larkin Villines. "Pretty Hez" was married to Minnie Edgmon. Nicknames had to be given to distinguish between the numerous Villines having same first names.)

Before the new church/school building was erected around 1918, there stood an old Beechwood building which would be replaced by the new one. Ab Phillips was one of the first preachers at the Old Beechwood Church. Martha recalls that he was a methodist and "sprinkled" her mother, Susie Villines Baker, at the church. Later, it served as a Baptist Church.

At one time the area at Beechwood was quite a thriving little community and had a post office.

Martha remembers that her mother told her about a Miss Lamb, who was one of the first teachers at the old Beechwood School. One day, Miss Lamb took a switch to Sam Scroggins (son of Richard and Tildy Keith Scroggins), a big fifteen year old who was causing a class disturbance. She could not hold and whip him at the same time and called on Bob Villines (son of Addison and Mandy Black Villines) to help her. Bob quickly leaned back, folded his arms and shook his head. "No, Mam', I cant' do that, he's my friend." Sam left and went up on the hill and threw rocks at the school all afternoon.

In the beautiful adjacent cemetery on a grassy knoll overlooking the Buffalo River and its valley are buried a large number of the first settlers of Newton County, a great many of which appear on the 1850 and 1860 U.S. Census Records for the county. There is another cemetery from early days where the dead were buried if the river was too high to be forded. It sits on a hill behind the "Old Hez Villines Place." That cemetery has been turned into a pasture and the grave sites, most of them unmarked, have returned to the earth once more. The grave of Piety Villines (the Negro Slave) is here and the only marked grave left.

Beechwood is fenced and flowers grow profusely throughout it. On Decoration Day, flowers, real and artificial, adorn every grave, marked and unmarked alike. There's always some old timer who recalls the day and place a certain friend or relative is buried, and for one reason or another, a marker was never erected except in memory.

WARRANTY DEED

With Relinquishment of Dower.

Know All Men by These Presents:

That we ... E. C. Clark and Flora Clark,

his wife, for and in consideration of the sum of ... No. Yor ... DOLLARS

to us paid by H. C. Villines and W. J. Villines Directors Dist. No. 9 and also the Methodist Church at same place.

do hereby Grant, Bargain, Sell and Convey unto the said District No. 9 H. C. Villines and W. J. Villines and unto their successors and assigns forever, the following lands lying in the County of NEWTON and State of Arkansas, to-wit:

The East part of the Southwest quarter of the South west quarter of Sec Twenty five Township Sixteen Range twenty three Described as follows beginning at the Northwest corner of the grave yard fence at a set stone and running North 35 yds to a stone 1 ft North of a Cedar tree 10 inches in (diameter thence west 70 yds to a set stone thence South 35 yds to a set stone thence East 70 yards to place of beginning Containing one half of an acre

TO HAVE AND TO HOLD the same unto the said H. K. Villines, and W. J. Villines as sumd Directors of said District and their successors and unto their heirs and assigns forever, with all appurtenances thereunto belonging

and WE hereby covenant with said H. K. Villines and W. J. Villines and their successors that we will forever Warrant and Defend the title to the said lands against all claims whatever.

And I, Flora Clark, wife of the said S. B. Clark for and in consideration of the said sum of money, do hereby release and relinquish unto the said Directors of said Dist No 9 and to the Methodist Church all my right of dower and homestead in and to the said lands.

WITNESS our hands and seals, on this 28 day of Feb 1919

Wm J Clark [SEAL]
Flora Clark
S B Clark [SEAL]

ACKNOWLEDGMENT.

STATE OF ARKANSAS,
County of Newton

BE IT REMEMBERED, That on this day came before me, the undersigned, a Notary Public within and for the County aforesaid, duly commissioned and acting S B Clark and D P Clark to me well known as the grantor in the foregoing Deed, and stated that had executed the same for the consideration and purposes therein mentioned and set forth.

And on the same day also voluntarily appeared before me the said Flora Clark wife of the said S B Clark to me well known, and in the absence of her said husband declared that she had, of her own free will, executed said Deed and signed and sealed the relinquishment of dower and homestead in the said for the consideration and purposes therein contained and set forth, without compulsion or undue influence of her said husband.

Witness my hand and seal as such Notary Public this 28 day of February 1919

J. G. Young

Filed for record on this ... day of Mar 1919 at 11 o'clock A M. and recorded on day of Mar 1919

P. L. Swain Clerk
By D.C.

Beechwood School & Church Deed

WARRANTY DEED
With Relinquishment of Dower.

Know All Men by These Presents:

That we ~~S. H. Clark~~ and O R Clark

~~his wife,~~ for and in consideration of the sum of ____ DOLLARS.

to Paid by Public

do hereby Grant, Bargain, Sell and Convey unto the said Public one interest for Burying purposes

and unto ____ heirs and assigns forever, the following lands lying in the County of NEWTON and State of Arkansas, to-wit:

Part of the South west South ½ South east ½ the part that is enclosed for Burying purposes & Said land ¼ Section Twenty five 35 — Township 16 North of Range 23 west Containing one acre

TO HAVE AND TO HOLD the same unto the said Public

and unto ____ heirs and assigns forever, with all appurtenances thereunto belonging.

And We hereby covenant with said public

that We will forever Warrant and Defend the title to the said lands against all claims whatever.

And I, O R Clark wife of the said S H Clark

for and in consideration of the said sum of money, do hereby release and relinquish unto the said public

all my right of dower and homestead in and to the said lands.

WITNESS our hands and seals, on this 8 day of February 1901

S. H. Clark [SEAL]

O R Clark [SEAL]

ACKNOWLEDGMENT.

STATE OF ARKANSAS,
County of Newton

BE IT REMEMBERED, That on this day came before me, the undersigned, a Justice of the Peace

within and for the County aforesaid, duly commissioned and acting S. H. Clark

____ to me well known as the grantor ____ in the foregoing Deed, and stated that

he ____ had executed the same for the consideration and purpose therein mentioned and set forth.

And on the same day also voluntarily appeared before me the said O R Clark

wife of the said S. H. Clark ____ to me well known, and in the absence of her said husband

declared that she had, of her own free will, executed said Deed and signed and sealed the relinquishment of dower and homestead in the said Deed for the consideration and purpose therein contained and set forth, without compulsion or undue influence of her said husband.

Witness my hand and seal as such Justice of the Peace ____ day of Feb ____ 1901

Ja P Casey J. P.

Filed for record on this 4 day of Mar 1919 at 4 o'clock P M. and recorded in

Beechwood Cemetery

Frank Villines' parents, grandparents, great grandparents, sisters, brothers and a host of other relatives rest at Beechwood.

I have carefully listed every marked grave at Beechwood, as of May 1, 1977. They are in the order in which they exist so that anyone wishing to locate a grave will at least have a clue of where to look. I began at the far left corner nearest the church and worked to my right with my back to the church, and then at the end of the rows I worked to my left. Some rows are not consistent but perhaps enough of a pattern was followed to find the grave one is seeking:

NAME DATE
Infant son of Mr. & Mrs. Doyle Williams 1936
Frances Elizabeth Youngblood 1909-1964
Unmarked — adult
Unmarked — adult
Unmarked — child
Velma Modena Youngblood 1943-48
James Victor Primrose 1923-1945
Christa Joyce Youngblood 1938-1940
Infant daughter ofMr.&Mrs.HenryPrimrose 1938
Infant daughter ofMr.&Mrs.HenryPrimrose..................... 1936
Infant daughter ofMr.&Mrs.HenryPrimrose..................... 1928
Unmarked —
Lieu and Sam Duty Lieu (1870-1954)
(a double marker) Sam (1866-1931)
J. Tal Villines (right beside gate) 1885-1972
Hezakiah Villines 1883-1930
Thomas M. Clark (Son of Sam & Orlena) 1883-1898
Killed by a falling log. Put in a silver plate but died anyway.
Ervin H. Clark (Son of Sam & Orlena) 1881-1899 (Ate too many peanuts)
Orlena Clark (wife of Sam Clark) 1853-1924
Samuel Clark 1851-1909
Clark child, son of S. D. & Flora Clark)
Three unmarked graves, probably more as space large enough for at least five graves
Leon Warren 1929-1938
A double grave in concrete rim enclosure, unmarked
Far right corner of first row, space for a number

of graves and believed to be where Negro Tim Villines and his family are buried. No markers.

NAME DATE
Albert Moore 1878-1887
Samuel Moore 1883-1885
John C. Moore 1827-1901
William Ross Arbaugh 1894-1958
Nora Ann Arbaugh 1886-1970
(Frank Villines' sister)
Unmarked (But Frank Villines knows that Bud Arbaugh, husband of his sister, Nora is buried here)
A. B. Villines 1854-1922
(Frank Villines' father)
Lou Villines 1887-1908
(Frank Villines' "own" sister)
Rachel T. Minton 1857-1888
(Frank Villines' mother)
Ira Villines 1879-1897
(Frank Villines' "own" brother)
Nancy Caroline Newberry 1857-1948
Martha Clark 1848-1896
(wife of J. M. Clark)
J. M. Clark 1841-1904
unmarked (this grave in front of Tal Villines' grave)
Babta P. Edgmon 1887-1888
(son of R. M. & A. E. Edgmon)
Robert M. Edgmon 1862-1891
(This man was born during the Civil War and he hemorrhaged to death (had tuberculosis).
Pearline Flood 1931-1955
Sallie and "Copie" Farmer Sallie1877-1945
(double marker) Copie1872-1936
Ersa and Harry Primrose Ersa1904-1972
(double marker) Harry1889-1958
No name but date of death1955
Unmarked
John A. Walker 1858-1942
J. G. Villines 1870-1943

Unmarked
Kansa Farmer 1910-1961
Jimmie Scroggins 1890-1959
M. F. Scroggins 1879-1958
Art Scroggins 1904-1929
Infant daughter of M. F. & Barshie Scroggins1907
Malissa Scroggins, wife of M. F. Scroggins .... date unreadable
Frank Villines (son of Copeland Villines) 1859-1894
Wilburn Villines 1914-1960
Lee Roy and Fannie Villines LeeRoy 1891
(double marker)Fannie1890-1976
Unmarked
Unmarked
Unmarked
Unmarked
Unmarked —.
Mary M. Keeton died 1901
Richard Scroggins 1829-1887
Tilda Keeton (daughter of Virginia Keith and
widow of John Keeton) 1842-1917
Seven unmarked graves in a line
Another unmarked grave
A. H. Clark (believed to be Abraham Clark) 1818-1890
Elvira Clark Patty 1854-1937
Jess Shroll (this book contains a vignette on
Jess and his life in Newton County 1886-1938
Mamie Shroll 1892-1919
A cluster of unmarked graves
Infant daughter of Joe & L. B. Villines 1883
Francis H. Villines, Son of J. & L. Villines 1880
Henry Villines, son of Jos. & L. M. Villines 1886
James P. Clark (infant) 1870
Sarah Young, wife of E. H. Young 1846-1871
Mary C. Clark died 1868
Eight unmarked graves
Thomas Franklin Johnsondied 1858

(This grave is the only one in the cemetery with a solid concrete slab covering it. Many legends surround it: During the Civil War a woman hid her side saddle underneath the slab wrapped in a quilt to keep the "mountain feds" from taking it from her; another story is that when a certain Newton countian killed another in feud fight, he did a dance on the slab to celebrate.

Josiah L. Patty, Co. M., II Pa. Cavalrynodate
(a Union soldier)
Five more unmarked graves
Maria Etta Patty 1870-1950
Gregory Scott Shaver, infant son of
Ron and Charlene Shaver 1969 Emma Louise Bums, 44 years old at her
death (daughter of Henry & Darcus Villines) 1976
Two unmarked graves
William Edgmon 1854-1865
Unmarked
S.Edgmon 1836-1861

(Aug. 10th)

Unmarked
F. P. Edgmon (a child) reading very dim 1866
James A. Edgmon (child) 1868
Hezekiah Edgmon 1860-1885
Samuel Edgmon (dim) 1831-1891
Unmarked
Bessie Duty 1897-1975
Eight unmarked graves
Martha Villines, 81 years old 1862

(This is the wife of the old patriarch, Abraham Villines. She must have been loved by everyone as there is a little story of interest: The Old Road from Ponca at one time went right through the cemetery and across where Tommy Baker, his wife Susa Baker and Virginia Farmer are now buried. The road came out right beside where Mamie Shroll is buried now. It seems that little four year old Frances riding a horse behind her mother, Mandy (Amanda, who was wife of Addison Villines) was sick and had been to see her grandmother, Elizabeth Penn Villines and Aunt Piety down the creek. She kept leaning over and Mandy cautioned her that she would fall if she didn't be still. She replied that she was trying to see if there was room for her to be buried beside her grandmother. This had to be Martha Villines, although not her real grandmother. Mandy hushed her and the little Frances rested her feverish cheek against the back of her mother. Four days later she died. Is she buried beside her "grandmother" in an unmarked grave? Virginia J. Keith (dim, could not read dates, but known to be very old as she is on the census records before the Civil War) the marker is broken

William Keith 1811-1842
(Oldest marked grave in the cemetery)
Four unmarked graves, very likely relatives of Virginia and William Keith.
A grave with a rock with initials M. K., nothing else.
Pamela A. Roark, 32 yearsofage 1866
Carrell Roark (child with no date)
Another rash of unmarked graves
Little Edith, daughter of L.G. &Rachel Young 1920
Four years old
Rachel and Lester YoungRachel1890-1938
(double marker)Lester1883-1960
Elizabeth Wilson died1915
John S. Wilson died1922
Son of J. H. & M. H. Knight (very old grave) no date Susie and Harley Farmer (still living but a beautiful marker (double) ready and waiting).
Jon Patrick Tougaw died 1968
Susa and Thomas Baker Susa 6-27-1874 - 6-6-27
Tommy9-3-1871 - 5-24-1929
Lorene House 91-1920 - 9-12-1920
Lettie Gibbons 1912-1915
Rebecca Cecil Villines 1826-1905
William Villines 1828-1875
Eliza Villines, wife of Marion Villines 1864-1943
E.M. Villines (Marion) 1861-1908
Ambrose Villines, (son of Eliza & Marion) 1884-1887
Rosie Villines, daughter of Eliza & Marion 1883-1901
Elizabeth Arrington (daughter of Copeland
Villines and wife of John R. Arrington) 1851-1901
Unmarked

Lillie Villines (wife of L. G. Young) 1882-1905
Other Lloyd Young (infant son of Lillie & L. G. Young) It would seem the
birth of this child was instrumental in the death of Lillie, his
mother) Both died in 1905 1905
Joel A. Villines, son of J. M. C. Villines (very dim, could not read date)
Another rash of no markers
At this point I stopped listing the unmarked graves as they were numerous and
I was getting tired.
Oliver Brewer 1818-1909
Betty Farmer (infant) 1922
Richie Farmer (infant) 1934
Joseph Villines 1871-1955
Almeda Vilhnes (wife of Joseph Villines) 1872-1904
Susie Villines (second wife of Joseph Villines
and daughter of Abraham Clark) 1885-1971
Francis M. Villines, son of J. M. & M. A. Villines1888
Margaret A. Villines, daughter of J. M. & M. A1863
(a guess as datenot clear)
Miley E. Villines, daughterofJeff & M. A August,1861
(died of smallpox four months after the Civil War began)
John A. Villines, son of Jeff & M. A 1863
(another victim of Smallpox)
W. M. Villines 1873-1882
Mary & Jeff Villines Mary1850-1917
(double marker)Jeff1832-1887
William & Lue VanCuren William1870-1925
(double marker) Lue1888-1969
Sarah & Walter ArbaughSarah1883-1956
(double marker) Walter1880-1955
Infant son of Mr. & Mrs. W. A. Arbaugh1934
ғ.B. Arbaugh 1928-1930
Frankie Arbaugh 1925-1927
Ruth Arbaugh 1909-1913
another Arbaugh (could not read dates)
Corp. Arie Arbaugh 1896-1921
(a World War I soldier?)
William Arbaugh 1857-1932
Gennettee Farmer 1880-1935
W. T. Farmer 1877-1964

Nancy J., wife of J. A. (veryold) nodate
John A. Henson 1848-1913

(doubtful date)

Harper (nothing else) nodate
Joseph Walker 1900
Virginia Brewer 1862-1935
Elzada Villinesdied1902
(daughter of Hosea & H. Patty Villines) I was told that she was the prettiest girl on the creek and had big plans to be married to young Sam Barnes, but died just short of her wedding date of typhoid fever.
Conrad Arbaugh Born1826

died 1901

Arbaugh (not readable)
Infant Arbaugh
Locille Keeton 1915-1952
A marked grave but too dim to read
A grave marked "Our Son" seventeen years old This grave is near the fence right in front of Clarence Clemmer grave.
Clarence Clemmer 1891-1908
Estelle Clemmer 1867-1940
Laurence Clemmer 1893-1954
Mary Clemmer Werner 1924-1972
A double marker —
Harriet & George VillinesHarriet1869-1898

George 1867-1901

F.Agnes Villines (baby) 1897-1897
Effie Villines 1895-1897
George Britt Keeton 1892-1968
Emma J. Keeton 1885-1945
Alfred Keeton . 1910-1941
Alfred Keeton (couldbeasonof above) 1932

18 years old

John Goodnight 26yearsold—died 1885
Alfred Keeton Co. D
2nd Ark. Cavalry nodate
Virginia Villines (infant) 4-30-1864
Another infant Villines nodate
Vestal, wife of Ross Villines 1915-1951
(There is a little wooden house built over this grave in the far right corner)

Doy Denver, son of J. H. & M. L. Clark 1896-1898
Two graves enclosed in concrete enclosure
Mary L. Clark & J. H. Clark Mary1872-1952
J. H. 1868-1945
Double marker —
W. I. & Alpha Villines W.I.1886-1973
Apha 1887-1963
James Villines, Son of J. A. & S. T. Villines 1888-1905
Double marker — Sarah & James Villines (This is "Beaver Jim", son of
Williamand
Rebecca Cecil Villines. A little vignette onhim
is in this book.) Sarah1855-1932
James 1854-1948

This concludes the listing of graves at Beechwood.

"All that lives must die, passing through nature to eternity
— Shakespeare

Hemmed in Hollow

We have not wings — we cannot soar.
But we have feet to scale and climb,
By slow degrees, by more and more,
The cloudy summits of our time.

— Longfellow

Hemmed-In Hollow is just what the name implies — a long, jungle-like hollow, hemmed in on three sides by mountain bluffs covered with luxuriant vegetation.

Frank Villines gave us a guided tour of this "Garden of Eden" near the Village of Ponca, (as the crow flies.) If the crow is not flying but traveling by something on wheels (and it should be with a four wheel drive), he can leave Highway 43 and take the Center Point Road down to the river and eventually reach Hemmed In Hollow.

We approached it by climbing over the mountain in the early spring. We made our way cautiously since several climbers and hikers have lost their lives in falls from the narrow limestone ledges.

A good soaking rain had fallen the night before and each bush and tree dazzled as the sun caught the clinging drops of water and turned them into a million jewels. Through the dense undergrowth, Frank pointed out the Buffalo River many feet below.

We followed a nearly invisible path probably made by deer and/or nature lovers. Several times our feet slipped on the dark, wet earth and rock and we had to grab at a sapling or each other to keep from tumbling headlong down the steep decline.

Wild columbine, bloodroot, star flowers, mountain iris and tall orchid-like flowers literally carpeted either side of our trail. There were many flowers I have never seen before nor since which apparently thrive only in Newton County.

I have searched many books on flowers and yet have not found some of those beautifully mysterious ones found there. It's as though God reserved them especially for the Ozarks of Northwest Arkansas.

115

In the fall, I expect to find another entirely different array of beautiful flowers at Hemmed-In Hollow.

Our surroundings were truly like a technicolor Tarzan jungle movie scene and I don't believe I would have been too surprised if the skimpily clad he-man-of-the-jungle had swung by me giving his famous yell.

We were completely captivated by the lush beauty around us and then Frank told us a romantic, but true, story about a one time resident of the Hollow . . .

A certain Irishman by the name of William Patrick O'Neill, weary of the world's pressures, sought a quiet, simple way of life and found his haven at Hemmed-In Hollow many years ago.

Hemmed-In Hollow is an abyss or chasm several acres in extent which geologists believe formed when the roof of an ancient limestone cave collapsed leaving a great pit-like opening in the earth, opened only at one end whereby the Buffalo River flows.

Colonel O'Neill, who served in the Navy at one time, was a polished old gentlemen, highly educated in the classics. He had a great love for the works of Shakespeare. He wore an impressive golden brown beard, and his eyes seemed always to be laughing. The natives called him the Hermit of Hemmed-In Hollow.

But he, in fact, loved people and appreciated talent of all kinds.

He built a comfortable cabin in the Hollow and planted flowers and a big vegetable garden for his wife, who spent a good portion of her time there. The Colonel was fascinated by flowers and often could be seen wandering aimlessly in search of a certain kind.

The O'Neills had six children and one of their daughters, Rose O'Neill, became world famous for her creation of the well-loved "Kewpie" doll. At one time in Germany alone, there were twenty-one factories producing this delightful little doll for the whole world to love.

Colonel O'Neill built a ladder up the side of the bluff as a short cut so that mail and supplies could be brought in. Otherwise, his cabin was almost inaccessible and reached only by climbing over the mountain and descending on the ladder or coming along a very narrow bench trail along the river. Even this trail was impassable when the river was in flood stage.

The stately old gentlemen found his refuge and spent his last days blissfully happy with his books, his memories and his family, who cared for his every need. When he became very feeble, he and his wife went to California to be near another daughter and the old Colonel died at the Old Soldiers' Home at the age of 102.

The little cabin either burned or rotted down. Erosion and time washed away the terraces where the multitude of flowers had bloomed gaily for many years. There are now no signs of human habitation . . .

I earn what I eat, get what I wear, owe no man hate, envy no man's happiness glad of other men's good, content with my harm.

SHAKESPEARE (As You Like It)

By now, we had reached the summit of the mountain and peered over into the Hollow. The hermit's ladder was gone and only a straight-down hundred feet or so greeted us. We then climbed down another side onto the narrow trail, slipping and yelling as we went and entered mystery-filled "Hollow."

It was not difficult to see why the Colonel had found it such a wonderful sanctuary. Still more varieties of flowers bloomed here and there. We counted Pileated Woodpeckers dashing about; the kind rarely seen any more. Squirrels scampered about and birds literally strutted their tiny jugular veins to entertain us royally with their song.

A pebble-bottomed creek, now dry, centered the hollow which serves as a relief when the Buffalo goes on one of her tangents.

We had almost reached the end of the hollow and were now a bit weary, but still fascinated by our surroundings.

We vowed to bring our lunch and water jug on our next trip, since it had taken longer than anticipated.

But what an experience! I shall never forget Hemmed-In Hollow and will come back. Before I reluctantly turned to go back to the noisy, confused "civilization", I stood quietly and listened: I could almost hear the Colonel's soft humming and a hoe clicking against the rocks as he worked among his flowers.

Where flowers are, God is and I am free.

— John Clare

A Place Called Lost Valley

Nature does nothing without purpose.

— Aristotle

Lost Valley is not really a valley at all, but a narrow gorge cut by Clark's Creek, an arm of the Big Buffalo River. Clark's Creek was named for the old patriarch, Abraham Clark, one of the early settlers in the area. The creek winds between the sheer cliffs of the "valley" for a mile or more until it emerges from a cave and falls into the waiting creek bed below.

Lost Valley was formerly a State Park, but was donated to the Federal Government by the people of Arkansas to be made a part of the National River.

I have seen and enjoyed the valley in each of its magical seasons:

Spring, with its promise of good things to come, casting a fairy like appearance on the moss covered rocks of various greens; dewy, early blooming blood root, dogwood, violet and wild strawberries blooming in profusion. Clark Creek is flowing from the spring rains and in places reaches the high banks bucking like a wild pony . . .

Summer, the "middle" season, like man in his prime, gives the best she has to offer: lush raspberries, blackberries big as the end of the thumb and others much to the happiness of the birds, squirrels and other wildlife populating the valley.

Fall, with towering oaks, maple and sumac sporting their brilliant colors. The paw-paw's strong banana like aroma. According to ole timers, the first frost will "sweeten" the paw-paw fruit.

Winter, with the many waterfalls frozen to immobility, barren trees white as bleached bones, has a beauty all its own. Soft snow slowly covers the valley floor of rocks and deep spongy beds of leaves and fallen hickory nuts.

Lost Valley lies in a very rugged section of the Ozark Mountains and was the home of Indians centuries before the early settlers began to arrive. The area is virtually untouched by civilization and is a natural wilderness spectacle. Eden's Cave above a waterfall by the same name is a worthwhile climb. In the summer, the cave is "air conditioned" and brings chills of delight

118

to a weary hiker. (More on this vignette on Clark Creek in Buffalo River Section.)

All the trails are well marked and there are quite a number of camp sites with water available. A ranger is stationed nearby to answer questions or offer assistance.

The unstable limestone bluffs along the trail at Lost Valley are extremely dangerous and hikers should avoid getting too near the edges. Otherwise, Lost Valley is a wonderful place to visit for the nature lover. It's beauty defies description and as Arnold Glosgow once said, "when something defies description, let it."

Center Point
(Popularly called Big Bluff)

Center Point Bluff, now often called "Big Bluff," is approximately 680 feet above the Buffalo River in Newton County. Under that spectacular bluff, on the winding river, the first Center Point School was built a hundred years ago. The school was so named (as was the bluff) because it was located in the "center" of the district, the center *point* of the district.

Many old timers had their first schooling there, including Frank Villines, who attended it in 1893. He says he didn't even have a book but learned from a wall chart. His teacher was Frank Carlton, one time sheriff of Newton County.

Gertie Evans Studyvin, whose grandfather, James Evans, helped build the first Center Point School in 1877, remembers the exact trail she took each day to get down the mountain to the one room school. Gertie says her grandfather, Jim Evans, came to Arkansas the year the school was built. At that time, he was a young man, whose trade was that of carpenter, blacksmith and grist <u>mill</u> operator, The mill was run by water power from Sneed Creek. Later the Buffalo flooded and washed away the <u>mill</u>. Mr. Evans also served on the Center Point School Board for many years. He and his wife raised ten children.

In later years, Center Point School burned and another was built three quarters of a mile down the "creek," and it was also called Center Point.

At about the time the first school was built in 1877, Frank Villines Grandfather, Copeland Villines moved under the Big Bluff at Center Point. He had previously lived on what is now known as the Ike Wishon Place. Copeland's place under the bluff became the "old home place." One of Copeland's children (one of twelve), William "Fishing Bill' Villines, was a Union soldier during the Civil War. Copeland found it necessary to leave Newton County during the war because of harrassment of bushwhackers and Confederate sympathizers. However, he returned after the war and finished his life below the bluff. He was married to Jincey Reeves Villines.

Big Bluff as it is called most often today, can be reached by turning off Highway 43 onto the Center Point Road (ask locally) and going approximately three miles down the mountain. When the foliage is on the timber, it's easy to miss the turn off to the bluff's trail, but in winter, one can look to the right and get a panoramic view.

Frank Villines recalls many gatherings of the young people on a wide bench of the Bluff. They would bring their musical instruments and play their hearts out. The backdrop of the mountains produced amplification incomparable to modem technology.

Call it Center Point, Big Bluff, Goat Bluff (see section on Little Goat Lady of Center Point), or whatever you like, but call it spectacular.

When I am weary and want to be refreshed, I thrust my thoughts to a bluff high above a wild and rugged river in Newton County where a cool breeze is always blowing. I am reminded of a bit of a poem by Robert Frost:
"Z have climbed the hills of view
and looked at the world, and descended,
I have come by the highway home, and lo, it is ended."

This picture taken in 1971 at Center Point Bluff (Big Bluff). Just below us straight down is the river and the site of the old Center Point School. Just yards from where Frank and I stand, two young men fell last year, one to his death. The bluff is over 600 feet from the river.

CENTER POINT SCHOOL 1910

The Center Point School was located in District Number 31 and was built facing Big Bluff. A good looking teacher, Alice Kilgore, whose father was Jackson Kilgore (her mother was a Lackey) taught in 1910 (the year of the picture) and was loved by everyone and was a "dandy" of a teacher, according to Frank's interpretation. Every young boy in the school had a crush on the pretty teacher. She married Blain Chafin. She is number 46 on the picture.

Those in the picture are numbered and the numbers correspond with the numbers above the picture. There were only five on the picture whom we could not identify (and Frank really gave it his best try).

1. Ralph Gibbons
2. Bill Gibbons' daughter Bill Gibbons' daughter
3.& 5. Ray & Faye Villines
4. Unknown
5. Henry "Goose" Villines
6. Coy Villines
7. Jessie Villines
8. Harley Farmer
9. Bill Gibbons
10. Dewey Villines
11. Albert "Bub" Villines
12. Georgie Villines
13. William Knight
14. Nora Farmer
15. Unknown
16. Unknown
17. Chester Knight's girl
18. Nora "Fisher" Villines
19. Minnie Villines
20. Chester Knight's girl
21. Millie "Fisher" Villines
22. Unknown
23. Abner Knight

24. Unknown
25. Lonzo Spencer
26. Mae Carlton
27. Burl Lackey
28. Cynthia Villines
29. Nancy Villines
30. Jimmie Carlton
    (peeping around)
31. Janie Villines
32. No number 34 —
    error made here
33. Linda Villines
34. Nora Bryant
35. Delia Villines
36. Josie Eoff
37. & 40. Chester Knight
    & baby
38. Susie Eoff
39. Jim Villines
40. Susie (Bragg) Villines
41. Frank Bragg
42. Lona Villines
43. Alice Kilgore

"Center Point School 1910"

Tom Thumb Spring

"Then shall thy light break forth as the morning, and thine health shall spring forth speedily . .

The Book of Isaiah

There is a cove in north Newton County which is hemmed in on three sides by the high bluffs of Gaither Mountain. It is the site of the well known Tom Thumb Cemetery and spring.

Long before the white man came to the area, a large band of Shawnee Indians lived in the beautiful cove and drank and bathed in the waters of the spring, which they believed had healing powers.

Over the years, by word of mouth, it became known that the spring was a panacea for all sickness. After the Indians left, early settlers came from all around and brought their ailing family members. It has been said that Abraham Clark (written on elsewhere in the book) brought his ailing wife, Sabra Ann Edgmon Clark to the spring in 1854 to drink the magic water, but alas, she died and is buried there but her grave has no marker.

It is believed that Elizabeth Penn Villines along with other family brought the consumptive Hezekiah to the spring in the hope of healing him, but he also died. Many believe that he is buried in the Tom Thumb Cemetery in an unmarked grave, but there are as many who believe he is not. This was approximately the year 1844.

About 1875 a Dr. T. J. Jayland owned the spring and promoted its features. Some believe the spring is named after the good doctor who was "no bigger than your thumb."

Records show that in 1880 the spring was owned by a Mr. Briscoe who operated it as a health spa. (Remember Aunt Lizzie Briscoe, the midwife?) Mr. Briscoe's son reported that after his father bought the spa, an old Indian returned and told him how his people had drunk from the spring for many, many years before the white man learned about it.

At one time it was estimated that a thousand or more people were living and/or camping in the Tom Thumb area near the spring. In 1892 only two families and some dilapidated buildings remained. Some say it was abandoned because the lots could not be purchased.

The spring is located on a bench which varies in width from a few yards to a quarter of a mile and goes around the cove. The water, clear and odorless has an alkaline taste. It was analyzed at one time and found to contain far more solid matter in solution than the famous Eureka Springs, Arkansas water.

I had the occasion to visit the spring a few years ago for the first time and browsed through the cemetery. I had a let down feeling when I saw the spring. It was almost filled in and the cemetery was in much need of loving care.

I closed my eyes and imagined a little doctor with a high topped hat running here and there filling bottles and buckets with water and passing them out to the sick and dying. I imagined also how the wagons grumbled as they pulled the steep hill loaded with sick passengers stretched out on mattresses in back, their faces filled with hope for a cure. Then I envisioned grief stricken families laboriously shoveling through the rock digging a grave for those who didn't benefit from the magic water.

The locale is a haven for birds of every kind and flowers grow profusely. The cove with its tiny spring struggling to rise above the green moss and mulch of leaves lives on. Now, the area is almost primitive and rugged as it must have been when the great braves of the Shawnee Tribe found the spring, tasted its water, nodded and spoke to each other saying that it had a strange taste and thought it was good medicine.

The roads leading to Tom Thumb are unmarked and it is easy to get lost, so it's best to ask locally for directions upon reaching Erbie Community where it is necessary to cross the "creek." The roads are very steep, crooked and all "one lane" and dangerous to the novice hill traveller. The scenery is breathtakingly beautiful and surely because of the scenery, a healing therapy begins taking place long before reaching the curative spring.

VII

... AND THERE ARE CAVES

.. All day the wind breathes low with mellower tone; thro' every hollow
cave and alley lone ..

> From the Lotus Eaters By:
> Alfred, Lord Tennyson

Caves are defined as chambers beneath the earth in mountains or on
mountainsides. Newton County has its share of caves, chambers and sinks,
some famous and lucrative such as the Diamond Cave near Jasper and the
cave at Dogpatch and its small tunnels. One of the largest known caves in
Arkansas is Beauty Cave located in Cecil's Cove in Newton County. The cave
has many miles of surveyed and mapped passages, and one room is at least
700 feet long. It houses some of the most beautiful formations of any cave in
the world. But because of vandalism, much has been ripped out and taken
away from the pristine beauty, and it is presently closed to the public. Plans
are being made by the National River authorities to eventually open the cave
to the public.

Hundreds of caves dot the mountainsides and many are probably still
undiscovered and unnamed except by the natives.

Frank says many of the caves have waterfalls and fresh water springs in
them and before the days of prohibition (and afterwards too) many stills were
set up inside these caves because of the good supply of water. A well known
still was operated by a John Dale for many years in the early days of Newton
County and was located at the head of Henson Creek. Under the natural rock
shelter a good spring of water was close at hand. Dale's prices were
reasonable for the time — 35c for large gourd full.

Caves have always been an important part of man's discovery of a land.
Because of a consistent temperature all year, they were frequently used for
housing for the Indians and settlers while they were building cabins. Even into
this century, the Henry Rush family lived in a cave after their home burned.

127

The large rock cave provided them with permanent shelter, where they suffered neither from heat nor cold. The cavern was one hundred yards long and was partitioned off and used for all the farm activities. Mr. Rush had a good barn lot, a place to keep his honey bees, a tobacco shed and a vegetable storage shed. But most importantly, a cool stream of water came out of the cavern floor furnishing them with water and refrigeration. Frank Villines has visited in the home and found it neat and attractive.

Caves were also used as storm cellars. Near the old Jeff Villines Place across Buffalo from the Clark homestead was a cave where Abraham Clark hid out during the Civil War. Later it was used as protection from the storms. Smoke smudged walls from candles and grease lights can still be seen in this cave and also in others along the river near homesteads.

DEVIL'S DEN

Deep in Cecil Cove northwest of the aforementioned Beauty Cave is a cave known as Devil's Den. Actually, this is more of a sink than a cave but unusual enough to mention. It is seventy-two feet deep and about 18 feet wide at the top and somewhat wider at the bottom. On the floor of the sink, there are several passageways leading off from the main hole, which have not been explored.

This cave is only a short distance up and across Cecil Creek from Beauty Cave but is very difficult to locate. As far as is known, it has always been called Devil's Den, but no one seems to know why. One old timer when asked why it was named Devil's Den, laughed and said, "Well, hits a long way to the bottom and iffen you'uns fell in it you'd have a *devil* of a time gettin' out." That's a good enough reason.

SLACKER'S CAVE

During the First World War and perhaps even during the Civil War, there were many who didn't believe in fighting for a cause for which they had no special concern. A travelling preacher encouraged them to stay put and not fight and so they hid out. Nowhere in the country is there a better place to hide out than in the caves of the Ozark Mountains. Fifteen or twenty young soldiering age fellows took their guns and headed up Cecil Cove and spent the entire war. Slacker's Cave as it was named after their "slacking" is up in the far reaches of Cecil Cove.

People living in the area would frequently hear their guns fired while they were hunting, but when the authorities came, the slackers just seemed to disappear.

The cave supposedly has a small opening and goes straight down for about six feet and then opens into a gigantic cavern back under the mountain. The slackers were able to disappear by pulling a rock over the small entrance after they were inside and could live there indefinitely by coming out occasionally for food.

DIAMOND CAVE

This cave was discovered one cold day early in the 19th century by pioneers Sammy and Andy Hudson and their sons as they were out hunting. Their dogs ran around the hillside after something they couldn't see. They followed the dogs for some distance when it was discovered they had entered a hole in the side of the mountain. They couldn't hear the dogs so they got together, lit pine torches and got their guns and knives ready for an attack by some dangerous beasts. They went down some two hundred feet to an underground hallway where they found their mortally wounded dogs. They went farther and came to two dead bears and some bloody tracks. They followed the track and came upon a wounded bear and had a fight to the finish. The bear went for the torches and put them all out. They fought for their lives in the inky darkness and finally came out for the better of it.

This Sammy (Samuel) Hudson is the same one who killed a panther with a butcher knife. (See Mining section)

The hunters had discovered one of the most beautiful caves known and today it is two miles of brightly lighted subterranean passages filled with unbelievably beautiful strange and delicate formations. The cave is located four miles west of Jasper.

The Hudsons still live in the Parthenon area and Dr. Hudson, the eminent thoracic surgeon invited me in his home. His home is the same house which his grandfather built before Dr. Hudson's father was bom in 1857, when they first settled near what is now Parthenon in Newton County. The house has been kept in a fine state of repairs and another house "built" around the older one. However, inside one can still see the beautiful workmanship of the old seasoned hewed logs, darkened with age, which have stood the test of time. The home is lavishly furnished with gorgeous furnishings of yesterday.

BAT CAVE

Another very famous cave in Newton County is the Bat Cave or better known, perhaps as the Saltpeter Cave up on Cave Mountain near Boxley. This cave was instrumental in providing "peter dirt" for gunpowder during the Civil War until it was destroyed by the Union Army in January of 1863. There were many saltpeter caves during the war and when the north closed the doors, the south made its gunpowder anyway.

George Villines, son of Jefferson and Mary J. Keeton Villines remembers hearing how the gunpowder was made. Jefferson Villines played an important part in the Civil War and it is imagined that he related these things to his son:

". . . I shall never forget the tall smoke stacks at the smelters; one was at the Henson Place and the other at the Casey Place above Boxley. (This would be the saltpeter cave.) In the days of the Civil War the Conferderate Army had established powder and lead ore smelters in which they processed gunpowder and lead for their rifles. During the Civil War the Union Army destroyed much of the factories but the men of the community made the smelters for years after the war. Lead Ore was plentiful up on the flat above Hez Villines Place.

This lead was broken and put into the smelter and made into bars of lead which was then cast into round balls for muzzle-loading rifles. Powder became available in the stores later but lead was free with but a little effort at the smelter. The large kettles used by the Rebel Army to distill saltpeter from Bat Cave was a curiosity to most folks at that time and still are because of their large size . .

Another saltpeter cave was utilized after Bat Cave was destroyed. It was quite a distance up Running Creek and very difficult to locate unless one was familiar with the terrain. It became quite an important spot before the war ended and signs of distilling the saltpeter remained until a few years ago. Although not as large as Bat Cave, the Running Creek cave nevertheless served a useful purpose. It has been told over the years that the Union Army tried in vain many times to locate that second saltpeter cave but the Rebel guerillas discouraged any entrance to the creek which was rugged and "rasperous" as one Union officer described some of the Newton County countryside.

Bat Cave on Cave Mountain is one of the largest known of its kind and has many rooms and chambers still being explored by spelunkers this date. At one time it was told there was a room so beautifully furnished by nature with delicate shimmering formations that it was awe inspiring to enter it with light. But unfortunately, vandals stripped it of every piece of beauty over the years.

There is also a room in the cave so large that it was used as a "dance hall." Young people met there for many years to hold weekly meetings and get togethers.

WARHOUSE CAVE

Warhouse Cave is located under a bluff at the head of Hannah Hollow. The cave is on Reynolds Mountain near Parthenon and was undoubtedly a busy place during the Civil War and was occupied by Rebel forces. It is so difficult to reach and almost impossible to find once the mountain is ascended and the right bluff found that only a few natives know of its presence. It has been told that guerrillas for the Rebel Cause stored goods in the cave which they "requisitioned" from the Union Army and also held secret meetings there. It is very near Little Buffalo River.

Old timers know of a gigantic rock which broke away from the rest of the mountains eons of time ago. It is known as Hannah Rock, named no doubt, after the people who homesteaded the area, as the hollow is named for them also.

The 1860 Census Records show that a fanner, Andrew Hannah, age 40 and his wife, Elizabeth, both from Alabama, were living in the vicinity with their one child, Carinda, a six year old girl.

The rock, it is said, was used as a garden by Elizabeth Hannah, who tilled it by day and climbed down a ladder built by her husband. She then pulled the ladder down behind her when the day's work was done to keep animals from damaging her garden. It is here under the bluff at the head of Hannah Hollow that leads to Warhouse Cave.

VIII

... AND THERE IS A RIVER, A NATIONAL ONE

The Basics

Since a river's life is so much longer than man's, no one has seen or will see all its stages of evolution. If one were asked where their river came from, they might say, "Why, it's always been there." Not true. Everything has a beginning except the Creator.

Just west of the Buffalo Fire Tower, deep within the recesses of the Ozark National Forest in Newton County, Arkansas, rises a river, whose beginning is indeed insignificant. It bubbles up with uncertainty from beneath a thick mulch of leaves, looks around and trickles awhile and finally gushes onward, and then has quiet spells in deep pools, and gallops off once more. This "off and on" river carries on thus for one hundred forty-eight winding, spitting, spinning miles, snaking its way through three Arkansas counties of unbelievable wild and lush beauty until it reaches the great White River on the boundaries of Marion and Baxter Counties. It is called *Buffalo*.

Buffalo is one of the wildest and beautiful free flowing rivers left in America. The battle of whether to dam or not to dam is finally over, and she will thrive and revive herself through time, the great healer, and continue to be "a natural."

On March 1, 1972, the river was authorized by Congress as a National River and is the first in this country. The responsibility for establishing this first national (sounds like a bank) was given to the National Park Service of the Department of Interior.

But let's go back in time some one hundred and fifty years or so and look at Buffalo as the first white settlers must have seen her. Frank Villines relates that his ancestors probably marveled at the size and strength of the Buffalo when they settled near her. In places, she was as wide as the

133

Mississippi River, but instead of being muddy, her waters were clear and sparkling.

The river, as always, served as the lifeline for the early settlers and life was profoundly affected by her erratic stages. Winters and springs almost always found her in flood stage sucking everything in her wake, leaving nothing but clean washed beaches and it took much hard work to rebuild houses, bams and fences. Even today, this happens, although she's no longer the rampager she was then. Frank recalls many times while he lived on the river how she flooded the narrow valleys and scraped every grain of topsoil from the banks plus all the fences, baby pigs and anything which could not hurriedly get or be gotten to higher ground.

Frank feels that indiscriminate timber cutting and cattle pasturing along the river has, among other things, left it vulnerable to "spreading out" and caused a loss of depth and momentum. Ole Buffalo needs time to "renew herself" and the National River is the answer.

The first settlers shared the bottom land with the Indians until the Cherokee Treaty of 1828 moved the Indians farther west. More settlers came and saw the land was good along the river and burned the cane bottoms and planted crops.

In the 1830's Frank Villines' great grandfather, Abraham, came with his caravan (discussed earlier) and they thrived well with the help of the river. From then until the 1920's Buffalo did her share to bring prosperity to the area as timber companies came and turned the gigantic white oaks into staves for barrels and thousands upon thousands of first class logs were floated down the Buffalo to become ties with which to build railroads to bind our country together. Even then, Buffalo had "national" interests.

Giant cedars grew abundantly along her banks and were cut and sent soaring down the river to be dispatched to the penny pencil companies. This brought another flight of good times to the area and old timers today recall the backbreaking work but happy memories of the cedar floats. A chapter on those floats appears earlier in the book.

As early as 1880 with the development of zinc mines, the owners began searching for ways to make Buffalo navigable. Transporting the zinc ore was a tortuous trip over roads so rough, it jarred the teeth of beast and man. The poor roads went up and down over mountains to Buffalo City, which was near the junction of White River. The nightmarish trips compelled the owners to find a way to use the river to get their ore to market. It was believed by many that the ore could be shipped down Buffalo on flat barges at least six months out of the year to Batesville. The other six months they would have to rely on getting it to market over the teeth-jarring "hills of purgatory" to Buffalo City. And some ore was indeed shipped down Buffalo, many tons of it.

A giant hunk of zinc weighing about five tons was mined at the Morning Star Mine on Rush Creek. They attempted to ship the "big rock" overland by wagon but it was too heavy for the beasts of burden. To the happiness of the mules, it was decided to build a big barge at Rush and the ore was loaded on and floated to the mouth of the Buffalo River, where it was transferred to a steamer and carried to Batesville. From there, it was shipped by rail to the World's Fair in Chicago in 1883.

There were many requests and much effort to improve the river so it could be made ready for steamboat navigation and much publicity was had, but nothing resulted from all the trouble. In 1896, steamboat Captain Will Warner plied the mouth of Buffalo for some forty miles with his steamer the Dauntless, and gave curious and startled hillsmen a free boat ride. The starry-eyed captain proved that the river was navigable at least part of the year and certainly deep enough for small steamers.

The publicity of the forty mile trip up Buffalo made history and caused much discussion and more efforts to make the river a possible trade route. After much investigation it was concluded that commerce on Buffalo did not warrant the expense of locks and dams and the dream died a quick death.

After all the cedar was cut and floated away, the area began to wither economically and some of those who had gotten used to the extra money in their pockets left in search of work and many farms went to pasture and woods. Following the second World War and maybe sooner, word of mouth told about the good fishing on Buffalo and fishermen came and went back bearing stories of the river's merits to their city contemporaries. Canoe clubs came into being and old Buffalo's charm was once more beckoning. But this time the allurement was not for a place to live where man could function without oppression, but for sheer pleasure and relaxation. But not all came for simple relaxation. Some came because of a weariness of spirit. More on this later.

After Congress passed the National River Act in 1972, Old Buffalo yawned and stretched and looked about and began to strut. Now, she was a National River and would be saved from destruction.

Excessive cutting of timber along her banks had begun the destructive cycle of erosion, sending the river in too many directions at once, none of which could be deep or meaningful. Frank says that even as short a time as fifty years (short for river life) ago, Buffalo had many holes almost anywhere along her nearly ten feet deep. Now that she has been "adopted" she will be nutured and loved and guided in the right direction so that one day she will return to her old self again.

One must not think that just because the river is a National one that her waters will be Red, White and Blue or that a statue of Uncle Sam will be at every bluff of every bend of the river. No such thing. Her waters will still run a translucent green, bucking and kicking in spots and smoothly going steadily on her way in others, past some of the most spectacular and mysteriously beautiful terrain in the United States. Nor will she be beaten into submission by dams, for that would take away her greatest merit, that of being wild and independent. Instead, she will be treated like a strong willed child who is also sensitive. This will amount to "managing" the river.

The Buffalo and her delightful counterparts, the mountains, woods, creeks and caves will have a "Big Brother" to look after them and that will be good for you and me and our children who come after us.

Frank's River, My River

Forget about the river being national, managed or what have you and picture if you will a man in the twilight years of his life and a woman in her middle years walking along the banks of Buffalo. What do they see and what are they doing here?

The woman is staring as though hypnotized at the water rippling over the shoals and glistening like so many diamonds in the sunlight. Now, she is writing something down in a book and speaking to the man beside her. He looks at her, his blue eyes twinkling and tells her another story about the river.

It's time to leave, but both seem unwilling. There seems to be no need for conversation as they look into the water and at the bluffs high above them. The man looks at the woman again and then at the sun quickly sinking behind a mountain and says something to her. She nods and begins to gather their belongings. It is the same each time they come to the "creek", so difficult to leave, but they tear themselves away and head toward home.

The man is Frank Villines and he has been here all his life. Fact is, he was born on the "creek", caught his first fish from it, set his first trap on it. He respects her now as he always has for the many things she has given him in his time of need.

I am the woman and each time I go to the river, I call it a working holiday. Nothing has ever lured me like this river, all the way from a farm in north Louisiana at least once each month since 1969 to spend a weekend or several days. Because of domestic priorities the time between visits gets shorter but it is my fondest wish to someday let my visits evolve into permanent residence since we have bought a place at Ponca, a little village near Buffalo.

The first time I saw Bufflao, she was shimmering in summer sunlight, beautiful and beckoning. I waded her and the clean pebbly floor felt good to my feet. As I gazed down the river and watched whitewater over a shoal beneath a towering limestone bluff, she snared me right then. I was her slave and she was and is my master. Never again have I been the same and each time I am near her, I am like one compelled and find it most difficult to leave her bank. There are rivers and there are rivers, but Buffalo, in my mind, heart and sinew is the river of rivers.

I shall never forget my first experience on the river with Frank. He is an excellent cook and had prepared "gritted bread" and placed fried ham slices between two of these "cakes." He had a thermos of coffee and the whole he placed inside a little shoulder bag. When it was time to eat, we sat on a rock and dug in. Nothing tasted better than that bread, meat and steaming coffee and to round out my feast, I searched and found a wild onion the size of a banty egg. Wild onions grow along the river abundantly and are quite large. Just another fringe benefit.

Frank showed me a place he calls his "office." He spent many happy hours there at that deep hole of water between Indian and Bear Creek and always came home with a nice mess of fish.

In the years I have known the river, I have walked her banks for miles searching for ginseng with Frank and my husband; I have floated her twice, once with my son and again with my family. The trip with my son almost ended in disaster as we were ignorant of her ways and moods. I have walked her banks looking for ripe papaws which smell for the world like bananas and are very delicious; I have fished her banks and was not disappointed. I have forded her many times with water almost under my armpits with my heart in my mouth, as my feet searched with uncertainty for a rock not so slippery. I have picked wild greens along her banks and gone home with armloads of poke salad, bear grass, wild lettuce and lambs quarters to be cooked in a black iron pot with a piece of ham meat.

Frank has never been very far from Buffalo and there is a friendly understanding between this man and his river. If she could speak to Frank, she might say something like this: "Remember, Frank, when you and your friends waded me and when I was low enough you'd carry your girl on your back across me so's she wouldn't get her dress wet? How you both laughed when your foot slipped and you almost fell!

"And how many times you came to me, discouraged and lonely and just being here with me would gladden your heart and mend things when you'd see a big ole lineside staring back at you through my clear water. Oh, the tons of fish you must have pulled from me, often with your heart in your mouth for fear that big one would get away.

"Say, you remember when you and that young friend of yours, Leness House were waiting on my banks for your girls. You'uns were going to a party. One of you had a little bottle of spirits, can't remember which one. Where you were waiting, I was mighty low and just had little basins of water here and there. But those little basins were plum full of tadpoles. Well, you'uns decided to take a little nip from that bottle but it fell from your hand and went crashing into one of those little holes of water. Almost at once, tadpoles began jumping out of that water like mad. Why, they was all stoned!

"Oh, I could remind you of a lot of things, Frank, but you don't need reminding as we've been friends a long time, about ninety-three years or so, eh? So much of your life has been shaped by my just being here waiting, so very much . . ."

Yes, Frank remembers many happy things about Buffalo. For instance the many times he and a group of friends had big fish fries on old Buffalo. He remembers Ed and Lizzie Minicus, the good-natured German couple who always came along. Lizzie could fry fish like something out of this world. There was no need to carry a lot of cookware along. Just a big black iron spider, a bucket of hog lard, a little meal, salt and the coffee kettle. When Lizzie took the golden browned fish from the sizzling kettle, she plunked them down on a clean flat rock. When the pile was about as high as it would stay, she called them to it. Plenty of fish, bread and hot coffee. That was all and it was plenty.

Later, someone would pull out their banjo and singing and laughter would echo against the towering bluffs as a group of young hill people indulged themselves in some real living, Newton County style.

Frank compares Buffalo with a woman because she is beautiful, charming and proud, but unpredictable. She can go on a rampage in a few hours and tear, rip and roar as she goes into flood stage. But as a man forgives a woman for her "nature" Frank forgave the river and loved her once more.

Many years ago, Frank mentioned to some of his friends that if possible, when he dies, he should like to be cremated and his ashes strewn along the banks of old Buffalo. To him, this would be the greatest final tribute he could pay to one that had nourished and entertained him for so many, many years. She is still a part of him and he a part of her — Frank's river.

I know that signs will probably not be allowed along Buffalo as it would detract from ber primitive look, but really, a sign needs to be put all along her pebbly banks which should read something like this:
WARNING! Partaking of the pleasures of this river and her environs can be habit forming to the point that you might not be able to leave.

Frank Villines today, busy in his shop.

The River Today

"A good deal of good can be done in the world if one is not too careful who gets the credit."

— An old Jesuit Motto

The Buffalo River encompasses some 132 *river* miles and is administered by the National Park Service, Department of the Interior with offices in nearby Harrison, Arkansas.

Much credit must be given to the Ozark Society which was founded in 1962 by a concerned group of folks who fought tooth and nail to preserve some of the natural areas within the Ozarks. With Dr. Neil Compton of

Bentonville, Arkansas as the leader, the Society had much to do with securing the status the river now enjoys. It was a ten year struggle and during that time they saw the need to save other natural resources within Arkansas. They are struggling to stop needless channeling of streams, damning of rivers, raping of forest by bull dozing, clear cutting and unnecessary spraying of hardwood. Their organization has brought about an acute awareness of the need to preserve this God given heritage in Arkansas and many have joined in their fight to keep it beautiful and natural.

Mankind *needs* a wild and beautiful river; a place to come and pull the cobwebs from his tired brain which civilization has encrusted there; a place to contemplate the reason for his being on this Planet Earth and to worship the Creator. He *needs* the quickening in his breast at the sight of a tall, sentinal bluff in the bend of the river, the beauty of a fern fall intertwined with trickling water; to smell the pennyroyal mint crushed by his foot and be refreshed by the uncanny cry of a pileated woodpecker.

Because these dedicated people realized this need, they fought and won. So many thanks to all who had a hand and a heart to save the Buffalo from destruction. For fear of leaving out any of those who worked so hard, I will not try and name all the "champions" to save the Buffalo River.

Since it seems no one has stated in simple language just exactly what is in store for Buffalo, this is an attempt to do so. There must be plenty besides myself who feel a need for this information. The natives at this point are fairly well tuned in to what is expected, with a few exceptions, and for the most part seem gratified by what is going on.

At first, as with any controversial issue, blood ran hot and angers flared. Some thought the government was taking over their land or stealing it from them, which of course, turned out to be absolutely untrue. Fact is, many and the term, *Most,* might be better, have realized a nice sum of money from land which heretofore barely netted enough annual income to pay taxes on it.

But even some of those who have been made better off financially by the "Park" are still not sure what is going on or what is proposed for this land they sold for a good figure. It will be a place for entertaining "furriners" but what else and why?

This is for those who really want to know what will "their" river become, for now, it belongs to *everyone.* In a sense, the landowners sold their property to the government, who is, in fact, the people, and she is giving it back to the owners to enjoy for as long as they and theirs shall live.

For the past five years, millions of dollars have been spent, not only for the acquisition of land, but for employing hundreds of professional people (many of these local) to come in and search out statistics, make recommendations and do tons of paper work to arrive at the best Master Plan for the river that can be had. Some of the finest minds have gotten together and worked out workable plans for organizing this Master one. Although the plan is now complete, more and more people will have to be employed to handle the soaring responsibility of managing the river.

From this day forward, Buffalo will be important, not because she has cedars for harvesting along her banks, or ores to be dug from her caves, but simply and purely because she is a river, and she is there, wild and wonderful.

Wilderness

. . What went ye out into the wilderness to see? A reed shaken by the wind? . .

St. Matthew 11:7

Try and imagine the first settlers along Buffalo worrying about preserving any of their new land for a wilderness section to be enjoyed by a later generation. It was wilderness, all wilderness and they could probably picture it as never being anything else. One never sees the need for saving something when there is such an abundance of it. Surely it would last forever. But sadly, it will not. Wilderness must be preserved, nurtured and petted and encouraged to last.

The National River people are obligated by law to keep and preserve a wilderness section. The Wilderness Act was written into the same act which brought about the National River. It would be hard to imagine a national river without a wilderness. Naught. It would have no more meaning than a city water works, just as sterile, just as meaningless.

A wilderness is defined as an area where the earth and its people are untrameled, where man himself is but a visitor who does not remain. No matter what he comes out to the wilderness to see, be it a reed shaken by the wind or anything else, he does not remain, or else it will no longer be a wilderness.

Along the National River there will be eventually 36,000 acres of wild and wooly wilderness. What an inalienable gift! Thirty-six thousand acres where man has not polluted nor fouled up things and where it shall never be done. It will be priceless heritage for all who come after us.

The three Wilderness areas will be the *Upper River Unit* at the very headwaters of the river, which is locally known as the Cave Mountain vicinity; the *Ponca Unit* which include 11,300 acres in the vicinity of the "Horse Ranch" Kyles Boys Camp and Camp Orr; and the third will be the *Lower Buffalo Unit* which will include 22,000 wild, woolly and wonderful acres of wilderness, all of which will be in Marion and Baxter Counties and go all the way to White River.

Grandiose things are in store for the visitor to these wilderness areas. There will be something for everyone from boating, swimming, hiking, horseback riding to bird watching and anything which strikes the nature lovers' fancy.

One day the towering cedars and stately oaks will grow as prolifically as they did on the river's banks 150 years ago. Our descendants will be able to see and observe animals and birds not seen anywhere else. The river will once again abound with fish of every species.

One might say, but what of the heavy visitation and usage? Will it have an opportunity to restore itself with so many thousands of feet trodding the "untrammeled" earth? That is why it will be managed and not overused. Traffic will be kept to a minimum in places of fragile grounds.

Frank told me that many's the time he sat in the cool of the evening on his front porch the forty years he lived in the Kyles Boy's Camp area (between Indian and Bear Creeks) and looked across the "creek" at the Big "A" on the bluff. Never once did he envision that he was living in a wilderness potential; that all the lands around him and up on the high bluffs would be preserved and protected solely for man's enjoyment. He shakes his head in disbelief.

This is only a small part of what the National River has planned for your river, Frank's river and my river, the Buffalo.

* The information on the wilderness sections of the river was provided by the Chief Interpreter at the Park Service.

Some Creeks Along the Buffalo

. . Far back through creeks and inlets making Comes silent, flooding in, the main . . ."

— Arthur Clough 1819-1861

Creeks and branches are loyal subjects bringing gifts to their king, the River bed. Without these "gifts" the King River would be just another creek.

The creeks along the Buffalo are generous suppliers of gifts of water and silt. Each creek was named either for those who first settled nearby many, many years ago or because of an incident along that creek.

Bluffs are the same and there are some interesting and humorous stories about the creeks, bluffs and coves along the river.

Frank Villines drew a map showing creeks along the river as he has known them for the 92 years of his life. He walked them, fished them, trapped them and drew from them sustenance necessary for more than life — for experience and a renewal of spirit. Each has a story to tell.

Perhaps there are those who will contradict how they were named or the exact order in which Frank placed them. But natives have a way of calling the same creek or branch by different names. I have pored over old maps and new maps for a pattern of how the creeks run and for the life of me can find none exactly alike or exactly as Frank has shown them. Therefore, this is Frank's version of how they run and how they were named. If he did not know some of them, I searched other places and sources for the best answers available. Some of the answers are strictly surmises.

The creeks will stop at Pruitt as Frank is unfamiliar with most beyond that point.So for the purpose of this story, we will talk about the creeks from the headwaters of Buffalo to Pruitt.

In all the years I have known Frank, I have never heard him refer to Buffalo as a river, but always the "Creek." No matter what he calls it, he always has a twinkle in his eyes when he talks about Buffalo.

REEVES CREEK

Up where Buffalo is just a mere trickle there is a creek and a mountain by the same name, Reeves. It is assumed that it was named by one of the early settlers in the area,
William Reeves who appeared on the 1840 Census. Addison Villines (son of Hezekiah), Copeland Villines (son of Abraham) and John Penn (brother to Elizabeth Penn Villines,) all married Reeves women and it is believed they were the daughters of this William Reeves who settled near the headwaters of Buffalo. When Newton County was taken from Carroll County in 1842, this area was referred to as Van Buren Township.

BEECH CREEK

Named for the many beech trees in the area. There is another Beech Creek on down the river. The upper Beech Creek at one time was called Sam's Creek for a B. C. Sam who settled there for awhile.

ARRINGTON CREEK

Frank does not show this creek on his map, at this location but the latest quadrangle map shows it. It was probably named for John Arrington (old) fondly referred to as Uncle John. Uncle John Arrington was a Justice of the Peace and hailed from North Carolina.

EDGMON CREEK

This creek was undoubtedly named for Braxton Edgmon, son of Samuel and Sarah Pierce Edgmon, who was a very early settler on upper Buffalo. There is an interesting story about the Edgmons who hailed from Tennessee. It seems that three Edgmon brothers married three Pierce sisters back in Tennessee. Johnson Edgmon married Rebecca Pierce; Thomas Edgmon married Nancy Pierce; and Samuel Edgmon (father of Braxton) married Sarah Pierce. Braxton Edgmon married Polly Casey and had a large family. They were very prosperous people. During the Civil War they experienced the loss of many of their loved ones.

MOORE CREEK

This creek merges with Edgmon Creek before giving itself to the river and was named after "the old timey Moores" who settled along it before the Civil War.

WHITELEY CREEK

In all likelihood, this creek was named for old Samuel Whitely since the 1850 Census Records show him as living in this area. He came here from Alabama but was bom in Virginia in 1797. He and his wife, Lucy, came to Arkansas while it was still a territory in about 1835. They built their home on a bench overlooking the Buffalo River valley south of Boxley.

Sam Whiteley was a southern gentleman and at every meal wanted the table set with linen cloth and napkins. He always dressed for dinner even though he was a farmer and grist mill operator. He enjoyed the nice things in life. It has been said that he was killed during the Civil War because he would not disclose to the bushwhackers where his valuables were hidden.

DRY AND RUNNING CREEKS

These sister creeks give themselves to the Buffalo at about the same location and are named simply because in summer Dry Creek is dry and Running Creek keeps on running. Also, up running creek is a natural millrace and another saltpeter cave which is high on a mountainside and was used after the big one on Cave Mountain was destroyed by Union soldiers. I have been inside this cave which is a unique place with drawings and figures dating back to the Civil War. I have walked up Running Creek several times for a long distance and find it one of the most beautiful places on earth. I wonder how many times I've made that same statement about places in Newton County?

It has been a legend that Confederate Rangers used this creek as a hideaway when the saltpeter cave was in operation. It would be a simple matter to become lost if one left the creek since there are so many caves and hollows to disappear into and the Union soldiers, unfamiliar with the terrain would not venture up Running Creek.

CLARK CREEK

On old maps this creek was first known as Farmers Creek, apparently for a David Farmer (on 1840 Census) living there. Fifteen years later, Abraham Clark settled on the creek (after Farmer had left) and the creek today bears his name. Abraham Clark has hundreds of descendants in Newton County today. He came to the valley in about 1855 and settled in the Beechwood area. It has been told that because he was a Union sympathizer during the Civil War, that it was necessary for him to hide out in a cave across Buffalo high in the side of the mountain. Smudges from his candles and pine torches still adorn the cave walls and that same cave was used as storm shelter for years by those living nearby.

Abraham Clark is buried at Beechwood where he was postmaster for many years. It was told that he built a beautiful walnut desk with pidgeon holes for mail and that some of his descendants still have it.

But the creek for which the old patriarch was named is now in the spotlight. It is only about three miles in length but what an unusual three miles it is.

It was necessary to do some question asking to learn why Clark Creek behaves in the fashion it does. The creek begins up Lost Valley, (see section on Lost Valley) a gorge which the creek carved and then after hiding itself among and under the rocks, it comes back to life in the big room of Eden's Cave where it drops into a breathtaking waterfall which is deafening in the enclosure. Then it curls itself out of the cave and makes another handsome waterfall just above Cob Cave and meanders on down disappearing now and then under the rocks into secret passages until it finds itself entering the Buffalo River. It has been said that it is so steep that it drops 400 feet per mile as it hurries to present itself to the King.

I was told the reason for it disappearing at times was because it was seeking the lowest channel to the river and in so doing goes through caves, crevices, sink holes and springs of water. This same phenomenon! happens on other creeks in Newton County. Tbis hide and seek behavior happens only when the creeks are not in flood stage for then they have nowhere to hide and must gush witb such momentum that even the wildlife nearby must put their heads under their wings or curl beneath their tails in order to sleep.

ADD'S CREEK

This creek runs down Highway 43 through the Village of Ponca until it reaches Buffalo at the low water bridge. Much colorful history is attached to this creek. It was named for a man who lived in the vicinity, Addison Villines, son of Hezekiah and Elizabeth Penn Villines.

At one time, Add owned all the land which is now Ponca plus much more around it. He was married to Lucy Reeves who gave him three children. She died suddenly and he married Amanda Black. He and Amanda had a large family, from which descended the mother of Martha Baker House.

Addison was an industrious person and when the Civil War began, he was harrassed because he was "well fixed" for those days. He joined the regular Confederate Army as a private in 1863 and served for several months before becoming ill. He later was connected with some Confederate rangers and had quite an exciting life until the war was over. As he was sitting around a campfire with his companions, an unknown assailant shot him and killed a man next to him by the name of Cross. Addison crawled and walked until he came to the porch of a woman he knew to be a Confederate sympathizer. She tried to get him to come inside and lie down, but he didn't want to get blood on her bed and told her he would just lie on the porch. He asked her to send for his son, Karr (Hezekiah) to bring a horse to fetch him home. He had been shot in the lower back.

Addison had many narrow escapes during the Old War but still lived to be an old man. He was loved and revered by all who knew him and the same feelings were held for his wife, Aunt Mandy. He sold much of his property to a mining company after the turn of the century and moved away.

CLIFTY CREEK

Frank says this creek is named for the Clifty family but doesn't know anything about them.

LEATHERWOOD CREEK

This creek is named for the many leatherwood trees along its banks. Frank recalls that he and his brothers used to strip away the tough bark of the leatherwood and make cow whips. According to Frank, old timers used leatherwood strips to cover chair bottoms, but it finally over the years became scarce and they switched to hickory which was more plentiful.

He tells the story of a certain family moving from one location to another and some of the children were misbehaving. The father pulled the wagon to a halt where Leatherwood Creek empties into Buffalo at the low water bridge near Ponca and told one of the older children to go over and break him one of those switches. The youngster grabbed hold of a leatherwood sprout and bent, twisted and pulled and made all sorts of faces trying to break it. He went from one to another but was unable to break a switch. He looked at his father and shrugged his shoulders. It is very likely that father was no longer angry at the children and everyone had a good laugh about the very tough switches along that creek.

Frank remembers there used to be lots of turkeys up Leatherwood and hunters rarely came home empty handed.

My first trip up Leatherwood was during the dead of winter when the timber was stark naked and icicles several feet long and inches thick hung like shining daggers over every ledge where water had dared to travel.

The temperature was fifteen degrees but the sun was bright and doing its best to warm us.

My teenage daughter and the family poodle, both of whom would soon be mothers, came along with me.

The creek was a silver wonderland with ice in every hole and crevice. Moss covered rocks were green stepping stones for getting from one side of the creek to the other.

We came to a ledge which extended out over the creek bed for about eight feet or so. It was decorated with icicles four and five feet long. We crawled between them and peeped out through silver "bars." It was warm there and we rested awhile on a thick carpet of leaves.

The poodle thought herself another Dorothy Hamel and skidded and skated on every hole of ice. When she misjudged and broke through, she dashed (embarrassed) up the bank and rolled in the thick bed of leaves until she was dry.

Giant oaks near the creek with most of their roots exposed, leaned precariously but still had the look and feel of total strength. Vines big as a man's leg wrapped snakelike all the way up to the tops of the trees, becoming smaller as they lost themselves among the branches above.

As I stood absorbing the scenery, wishing I could stay forever, a big Lord God swooped down into a tree just yards away, his plumage bright in the morning sunlight. We stood transfixed as we stared at each other before he decided he had better things to do.

I asked Frank once why the pileated woodpecker was called "Lord God." He smiled and said the first time some fellow in these parts saw one he didn't know what it was and said from utter amazement at the sight of the foot and a half long bird: "Lord, God, what a bird!" The name stuck.

Walking Leatherwood is not easy when the creek is running full, and we had to cling to tree roots, small trees and rocks (we hoped were stable) to keep out of the creek. We didn't feel like getting dunked in ice water since rolling in dry leaves just wouldn't get it for us as for the poodle.

Leatherwood reminds me a little of Hemmed in Hollow as the creek bed is wide in places and narrow and rough in others.

My daughter rested on a sunny bank while the poodle and I went tripping up the creek to investigate a large rock bed. The solid rock area must have been thirty feet wide and at least that long. It was like a stage and its rocky ledge formed a horseshoe effect around which the water was deep and clear. Behind me the creek had disappeared under the bed rock as it does frequently on Clark Creek, and I went on until I found it once more.

Frank tells me that the old fields along the creek were probably farmed by some early settlers, the Richard Scroggins family. I wonder if he was the one who sent for the leatherwood switch.

As we started to leave, Leatherwood whispered to me to come again in another season and go all the way to her head. I'm already planning what I'll carry along in my backpack.

STEEL CREEK

This creek was named for George Steel, a very early settler (1847) who hailed from Illinois and farmed the bottom along the creek that was named for him. His wife, Nancy, was bom in North Carolina. In 1850 they only had two sons but by the 1860 Census they had had four daughters bringing their total to six. All the children were bom on the creek.

It has been said that George Steel was a Colonel in the Union Army which seems a strange statement since he lived in "Confederate country" on upper Buffalo. Steel Creek was said to have a deposit of ricb lead ore near a roaring spring which could never be found in later years. Frank Villines said he spent many days searching for the Steel Creek Ore.

A newspaper clipping dated October 31, 1861 (Arkansas True Democrat) stated that a Colonel Steel from Newton County brought five hundred pounds of lead to Johnson County and sold it for thirteen cents a pound. The lead was smelted out of a log heap and he told them he had several tons of very rich ore ready for smelting. The clipping went on to say that Colonel Steel with a proper furnace could supply tbe Confederacy and there was no doubt that the lead mines in Arkansas were equal in extent and richness to those of Missouri. Wonder why Colonel Steel was in the Union Army and selling his lead to the Confederate army. Many strange things went on during that "Old War."

SNEED CREEK

Sneed Creek was surely named after the very early Sneeds who came but didn't stay in the county. Sneed Creek can be reached by going down the Center Point Road (ask locally) for about three rough and rocky miles almost straight down. The creek is where some of the early Villines camped when they discovered the Garden of Eden which is now Newton County. The area so captivated the camper Villines that they went back and told their kinspeople about it and they soon came.

About a half a mile or so above the creek's mouth, it travels over an expanse of bedrock at least a hundred feet wide and some four hundred feet long. The rock is smooth enough for a dance floor and is known as Rocky Bottom.

INDIAN CREEK

No doubt named for the Indians living along it. No one seems to know.

BEAR CREEK

Bears once inhabited this area. Frank tells many stories about Bear Creek as he lived forty years between it and Indian Creek. One wonders if this is the same Bear Creek in the very old records where at one time a Dr. Alvah Jackson in the 1830's employed sixty men in a bear oil rendering plant. There were 25 barrel makers, 25 bear killers, 5 rendering plant operators and 5 more boat operators. The plant flourished for 4 or 5 years at the mouth of Bear Creek in Carroll County (later Newton) in 1830. Might or might not be the same Bear Creek.

SHOP CREEK

Shop Creek was so named because of a blacksmith and repair shop located at its mouth. There is also a Dry Shop Creek which was so named because it was dry most of the time. The blacksmith shop was most likely run by Andrew J. Clements, a young blacksmith born in Missouri who lived in that area with his wife, Licenda and their three sons, John, William and Joseph, all bom in Arkansas. The hollow which he farmed was named for him and is so called to this day, "Clements Holler."

HICKMAN COVE CREEK

This one is bound to have been named for that old timer, Caleb (Calip) Hickman, who hailed from Tennessee and was a farmer according to the records. He lived with his wife, Nancy Jane Atchley Hickman and five children, William, Daniel, Angeline, Sarah E. and Rachel, all bom in Tennessee except the last two.

CECIL COVE CREEK

The Cecils for whom this creek and cove were named hailed from Tennessee. The creek was named for Joseph Cecil who lived up the cove with his family. Solomon Cecil, Joseph's father, came to Arkansas, but it is believed that he did not stay long. He was among that wagon train travelling to California who fell victims to the Mountain Meadows Massacre in 1857. However, Solomon was not with the group who split from the train. He and his clan went on to California.

Jim Cecil Hollow is named for one of the Cecil's who lived up that hollow. The 1850 Census shows a Jim Cecil living with the Flin Family, but it is not certain this is the same Jim Cecil.

Joseph Cecil's son, John, was Sheriff of Newton County for two terms and was well liked by everyone until the Civil War. John stayed with the South and this caused his many prior friends to be his enemies. He was known by those who loved him as a loyal captain in the irregular army of the Confederacy, commissioned by General Thomas Hindman, but those who were for the Union, tagged him a bushwhacker, John's brother, Sam, was a Union soldier and was instrumental in leading the Union troops to his brother's outfit in the Limestone area, where most of his men were killed, but John escaped.

Joseph Cecil and his wife, Margaret, are buried at Cherry Grove Cemetery.

MILL CREEK

This creek is a frisky little stream so named because at one time there was a grist mill located at its mouth. The creek mothered one of the first water powered grist mills to be built in Newton County. It was built by a Peter Bellah about 1840 on the location where Marble Falls (Dogpatch) is now located. Over the years, the mill was owned by several people, each reconditioning the mill to last a few more years. It finally became one of the best mills and cotton gins around and at one time was owned by Absalom C. Phillips. Below Mill Creek's waterfall was located a thriving sawmill and for a period of ten years or so there was a lot of activity up and down the creek. The area is known to many as *Wilcockson.* There are many mineral springs which caused it to be something like a health spa many years ago.

During the Civil War the area where Marble Falls is located was the site of a bloody ambush of six young Union soldiers and sympathizers. Many felt it was the work of Confederate bushwhackers while others felt it was the work of a lone man holding a bitter grudge for the families of some of the men.

Today, Mill Creek begins at the famous Dogpatch USA, drops over Marble Falls and keeps onward until it reaches the Buffalo River where it surrenders itself just below Pruitt.

154

HARP CREEK

Harp Creek becomes married to Mill Creek before giving itself to the Buffalo River and was named for the many Harps who lived in the area. The 1840 Census Record shows the following Harps living in the Upper Buffalo River area: Sampson Harp, William Harp, Samuel Harp and Ichabod Harp.

AUSTIN CREEK

This creek according to Frank, is near Shop Creek, although I cannot locate it on any map I have seen. In the 1840 Census there was a David Austin living in the area and he is probably who the creek was named for. He does not appear on later Census records, so he was one who kept moving westward.

The creeks described here reflect Frank's knowledge of them, plus some research of my own as to how they were named with a fragment of history about them.

There must be literally hundreds of creeks and branches along Buffalo, each reeking with history and color, but alas, they are strangers to me and to Frank. Perhaps one day we shall meet and I will be able to write something about them, too. If not, surely there will be other Frank Villines and people like me just itching to leam more about that "Creek." Together they will be able to create something about the creeks *beyond* Pruitt. I just know it.

IX

TALL (AND NOT SO TALL) TALES...

Tall (And Not So Tall) Tales

For entertainment and probably as a deterrent of bad behavior, the old women of the hills were the very best story tellers. Most of the stories had a small flicker of truth exaggerated to the enth degree to the delight and chills of the youngsters.

There was an old lady known as Mrs. Cross who went about to people's homes helping in time of child birth or sickness. She wore long heavy skirts and had her hair pulled back in knot on her neck and a cotton bonnet pulled snug down around her shoulders. At night after chores, she would reach up on the fireplace mantle and get her little clay pipe and dip it ceremoniously into the hot ashes to light it. She took her work worn, littlest finger and pushed everything down just right before lighting and puffing away and pulling the big heavy rocker nearer the fire. The children scampered into a little huddle around her chair making noises of fear and excitement.

Mrs. Cross would clear her throat, take a long drag on her pipe and begin. As she got into her story, the children got closer and closer together. No one wanted to be near the window and the cracks in the puncheon floor seemed to get wider and wider as her story got scarier and scarier.

Mrs. Cross wasn't the only story teller as they were numerous and many Ozark folk tales began in just such a setting.

THE HAMBRICK KNOB BABY

Many years ago during the Civil War, there were very mean and ruthless men who went about the country <u>killing</u> just for the fun of it. Their hearts had been hardened by their losses of loved ones and possessions. They were like animals and were known as "bushwhackers" or "breshwhackers". These men were not for either the North or the South, though each side thought they were and survived each day by depriving some farmer of the family's supper.

Just across the county line near Gaither, there is a big knob and a man and his family lived there at its foot. Their name was Hambrick and so the big knob was called Ham- brick's Knob. Now, Mr. Hambrick was what they called neutral and did not wish to be associated with either side. It was a known fact that he had food hidden in some of the caves in the area. The bushwhackers came one evening just before sundown. It was told that they tortured the man and tried to get him to tell them where he had his food and money hidden. When he refused, they took him and his young baby upon the Knob while the wife screamed and pleaded with them. They hung Mr. Hambrick from a nearby tree and threw him in a shallow grave. Rather than waste a bullet on the baby, they threw it alive into the grave with its dead father and buried them.

About here in the story, the grannie woman would dip her pipe once more for another light while the children, frightened almost out of their wits looked with wide eyes toward the window.

The legend has it the baby, though dead, continues to cry every night about the time it was thrown into the grave alive.

For years when hunters or travellers neared the area they declared they could hear the baby crying. Two brothers were hunting squirrel in the area when one of them heard the baby cry. They both began running lickyty split and ran for ever so far before the other one asked why they were running.

THE PANTHER AND THE HONEY

Once a young woman by the name of Mrs. Reynolds lived up on Swain Mountain. She decided one day to go and visit her lady friend who lived about three miles away. Her husband helped her saddle the horse and bid her goodbye.

After her visit she started to leave and her friend's husband had just robbed his bee hives and told her he would fix her a plate to carry home with her which he did.

Mrs. Reynolds rode side saddle as was the custom for women in those days and put the honey in her lap.

It was getting rather late and Mrs. Reynolds was anxious to get home, but her horse kept being spooked by something. Mrs. Reynolds felt like eyes were watching her from every rock and ledge in the mountains. The whippowhills had already begun their chants and she heard a big bob cat over on the next ridge and hoped her husband remembered to put up the chickens.

She scolded herself for staying so late and looked down at the fresh honey which was beginning to be a nuisance as she wanted to hurry. Then she smiled as she thought how good it would be with hot biscuits and churned butter and how her husband would enjoy it. She got a better grip on the plate and urged her horse to hurry.

Still feeling uneasy, she looked from right to left. Suddenly, chill bumps rose up her spine to under her bonnet as she heard a scream and looked up just in time to see a huge panther on a ledge over her. It jumped and the horse lunged causing the panther to land on its side. Mrs. Reynolds threw the honey plate at the panther, slung her leg over the horn of the saddle and the horse flew like wind toward home.

Upon arriving, she was almost in tears she was so frightened and explained to her husband what had happened. Her husband said the panther probably smelled that fresh honey and had been stalking her for a long time. He took his dogs, a gun and fresh horse and went back to the spot she had described while she went inside and bolted the heavy door.

He came back and shook his head and handed her the honey plate which had been licked clean as only a member of the cat family can lick a plate. He said he couldn't find tracks and the dogs didn't pick up his scent. They looked at each other in wonder. She saw it and knew it was a panther but why was the only evidence the clean plate. That night Mr. and Mrs. Reynolds locked up their chickens and put the pigs in the bam for safekeeping while their dogs barked at something in the darkness. Probably a big cat looking for more fresh honey.

THE LEGEND OF SAM'S THRONE

The Ozarks have their legendary characters and many of them are not so farfetched as others. Such was the case of Sam Davis, bom about 1795 in North Carolina. He migrated with his wife, Patsy, to Big Creek in Newton County. He was probably one of the greatest bear hunters in all of the county. In fact, as the story goes, he killed such great numbers that he rendered their oil and shipped it by ox team to St. Louis. He became wealthy and was the only slave holder on Big Creek. He was a most industrious man and invested his wealth. At some point in his life, he had such a mania for making money and reforming tbe world that he lost his mind, or at least, that is how the story goes.

Some say he was a genius who snapped, while others say he was a mean man who lost his mind over money and religion. Legend has it that he was a great Bible Scholar who wanted so fervently to reform the world that he lost his mind.

There is a very long mountain located on Big Creek (east) which is very interesting geographically. Its summit has an area of about one half acre or so with very good soil. It was covered with timber and almost inaccessible except by a deep slot on the west side which was only two feet wide. One had to climb through this crevice or slot and up the mountain.

Sam chose this spot for his throne. He cleared the mountain top of all timber except one pine and one oak and planted the whole mountain top in peach and apple trees. There is a remarkable feature of the location of Sam's throne in that even though it has a narrow base and elevated crown, a good spring of water is on top. Sam retired to his "crown" and drank from his spring and preached to the valley below, shouting his sermons for mankind to repent.

He believed that he would live a thousand years and then would preach for eternity from his throne.

The old man lived a long time and the bears destroyed his fruit trees and the Civil War began and devastated the rest of his dreams. But he did have enough mind left to hide his money and bored holes in a long cedar block and placed gold coins in these and then drove pins upon them. Many searched for his wooden banks but could ne<ver find them.

At times it was necessary to confine the old man in chains to protect him from himself. Many a story was told by grannies to wide eyed children about how the old man would break his chains and come running and screaming down the mountains, his chains rattling.

The story is that one day Sam in one of his better moods, hitched up a team and put all his belongings in back and started down the mountain. He was never heard from again. Some say he was murdered for his money he had in the wagon.

The 1860 Census shows Sam Davis as being 65 years of age and living with a Mary Criner, a widow with several young children. It shows his status as "insane." It is unknown who Mary Criner was to the old bear hunter/preacher.

It was told that he and Patsy had one son, Richard Davis, who became as great a bear hunter as his father, but he died a young man.

One wonders if Sam were alive today would he be chained for his radical beliefs, his wild dreams and lofty impressions? It's almost a cinch he would be called a revolutionist or activist and given a high place in this society, But then, over a hundred years ago he was classified in the U.S. Census Record as "insane."

". . . Wild tales to cheat thee of a sigh Or charm thee to a tear . . ."

— W. G. Wills

X

The New Breed

"Attempt the end, and never stand to doubt;
Nothing's so hard, but search will find it out . .
— Robert Herrick's Search and Find.

Today, there are new *pioneers* in Newton and other Ozark counties. "The New Breed", I call them, are most often young and intellectual people who have "migrated" to the hills. They, like the early pioneers are searching for a better way of life.

They are coming in droves in pickup trucks, Volkswagens and some afoot with heavy backpacks. They have heard of this "Mecca" where the terrain is beautiful, the air free of pollution and in places land can be bought for a reasonable figure.

The New Breed have not come to shove and afflict, but they come to be a part, almost an unobserved part where they can make a simple living from the good earth and have the peace so longed for by us all.

They are nutrition minded, and are planting gardens, herbs and organic goodies. They have their sights set on things of real value. It is not their wish to waste the energies of Planet Earth and are reading books on health, natural childbirth (without doctors) and hiking. They walk much of where they go as they are aware that the automobile has made us all invalids.

A Newton County lady told me she was skeptical of them at first and thought them "hippies" with long hair and to her the word "hippie" was synonymous with parasite and laziness. But one day several came to her and asked for work. She showed them a field they could clear. Men and wives jumped in and worked in the heat all day and did her a good job. She asked them how much she owed them and they pointed to her flock of goats and asked for a milk goat kid to raise for their milk supply. She was pleasantly surprised. Later she asked them to come to her church and they came with intruments they had carved and strung themselves and the beautiful music added a new dimension to the services. She told me she found them to be sensitive, intelligent and very industrious.

This is true of most of this New Breed. Naturally, there are exceptions. As Frank told me, there were families in his neck of the woods on the "creek" who had their health and land and still had nothing. He said that kind will always be around.

Just as the first Villines settlers on Sneed Creek saw it a good place to settle and raise a family, so must this new class of pioneers feel. These people have a right to find themselves and to get away from oppression if they desire. Their hair is long (and isn't everyone's almost?) but their hearts and minds are willing to work long, hard hours to realize their dreams.

The New Breed are not all young (in years). Some are young at heart but parents of adult children who have decided to retire early in the Ozarks and who have exchanged their other way of life for one of peaceful living.

The new breed are fervently aware that the land should not be raped by indiscriminate cutting of timber. Instead many of them search out fallen trees for wood and let the big oaks increase their girth until they are once more as large as they must have been 150 years ago. They know not to dig every sprig of ginseng or golden seal but to let it grow to its full maturity.

They are interested in seeing the Ozarks as they once were. The natives are slowly accepting this new breed and it is my hope they all will soon understand their motives and stop judging by their methods. That is why the new pioneers are so happy about the National River and the lands along it as they know it will not be destroyed by the sophistication of "civilization." They are trying to buy small plots of land outside the National River boundaries as close to nature as they can get and I say more power to them.

These new people in the Ozarks, and more particularly in Newton County are in my opinion, pioneers in reverse. They don't have to carry guns to protect them from wild animals, but there are still things they must avoid in order to survive.

The few exceptions who want only to *take* from the land and give nothing in return (and they also might have long hair) will eventually be weeded out and discouraged from staying by those who know a good thing when they see it.

Photographs

Frank Villines and a baby catfish
from Buffalo — about 1955

Jackson and Calvin Eoff
(brothers of Frank's stepmother)

Claude Harp and Delia Villines

Frank Villines & George Arbaugh (standing)
Tom Harp, Jim Jamison & Lester Young — about 1913

Louis House, Bill Lackey, Leness House &
Daniel Boone Lackey — about 1913

John Caulderhead & Frank Villines

Elzie Villines, Frank Villines & Lester Young and a Simmons boy.

Frank Villines (standing)
Bill Lackey & Eulas Kilgore

Frank Villines & Rachel Newberry

Lester and Rachel Young

Faye & Sarah Villines (Frank's half sisters)

Frank Villines and Caroline Newberry (Frank's maternal aunt) and Caroline's
sons, Albert & Onnie Newberry

Walter Wishon (Son of Milas & Lizzie Keeton Wishon)

Delia and Nora Villines (Frank's half sisters)
and Delia's husband, Jess Thompson and children

Dewey Villines (Son of Frank "Fisher" Villines) and Dorothy Kilgore

Rosetta (Etta) Villines Henderson and children, Bonnie & Ford.

Frank Villines in his twilight years
and my grandson, Jason in the early spring of his. 1977

Index

RUSSELL Sam, 31
SCROGGINS Richard, 109, 151
SCROGGINS Sam, 104
SCROGGINS *Tildy* Keith, 104
SHROLL Jess, 70, 71, 109
SICKLES Van, 89
SIMMONS (first name unknown), 91, 170
SIMS Betty, 75
SIMS Louis, 75
SOUTHERLAND Dr. Henry, 63
SOUTHERLAND Elmer, 88
STAFFORD Mrs. Carroll, 69
STEEL George, 151, 152
STRICKLAND Minnie, 4
STUDYVIN Gertie Evans, 63, 120
SUMPTER John, 80
THOMAS John, 80
THOMPSON Tim, 91
VILLINES, 21, 56, 57, 68, 69, 70, 71, 98, 100, 103, 104, 114, 120, 130, 147
VILLINES Abraham, 5, 18, 110
VILLINES Addison, 110, 146, 149
VILLINES Bell McCracken, 68
VILLINES Bob, 104
VILLINES Charley, 23
VILLINES Copeland, 109, 120, 146
VILLINES Coy, 122
VILLINES Cynthia, 123
VILLINES Delia, 123, 167
VILLINES Dewey, 122, 174
VILLINES Elizabeth Penn, 16, 21
VILLINES Elzie, 170
VILLINES Erma, 75
VILLINES Frankie Henderson et al, 31, 32

VILLINES Freeda, 75
VILLINES George, 113, 130
VILLINES Henry, 122
VILLINES Howard, 75
VILLINES Ira, 108
VILLINES James, 114
VILLINES Jane, 75
VILLINES Jefferson, 9, 104, 130
VILLINES Jenny Eoff, 22
VILLINES Jessie, 69, 122
VILLINES Jim, 123
VILLINES Jimmie, 60
VILLINES Jincy Reeves, 7
VILLINES John, 13
VILLINES Linda, 123
VILLINES Lou, 29, 108
VILLINES Lucinda Cecil, 68
VILLINES Mandy (Amanda) Black, 65, 104, 110, 149
VILLINES Marie, 75
VILLINES Martha, 110, 111
VILLINES Mary J. Keeton, 130
VILLINES Millie, 122
VILLINES Minnie, 122
VILLINES Nancy (Tim's wife), 11, 123
VILLINES Nancy McKissack, 6
VILLINES Nora, 173
VILLINES Nora, 122
VILLINES Perry, 75
VILLINES Piety, 20, 21, 104
VILLINES Ray, 72, 76, 77
VILLINES Rebecca Cecil, 10, 16, 19, 56, 111, 114
VILLINES Ross, 2, 53, 113
VILLINES Ruby, 75
VILLINES Virginia, 113
VILLINES Waymon, 18
VILLINES William, 111

Epilog

I'll never forget the time I met Frank Villines and looked into his twinkling blue eyes and felt his firm hand shake. He asked me point blank: "What'd you come to Newton County for — to die?"

I've given his question a lot of thought since then, and after spending a great deal of time in the Ozarks of Northwest Arkansas, I think I understand his question: There is no place on earth so grand to live and certainly no grander place to die.

James Franklin Villines at the age of 94 years, left this world in January of 1979 and took his place in Heaven. As this book goes to press, for the fifth time, it is springtime in the Ozarks. I can almost hear the chains rattling as they are placed about Frank to hold him so that he won't try and return to THESE HILLS, MY HOME.

THE END

www.ingramcontent.com/pod-product-compliance
Lightning Source LLC
Chambersburg PA
CBHW030443290526
45786CB00001B/427